Table Of Contents

Chapter 1: Exploring Your Sensual Desires and Fantasies

Understanding Sensuality and Fantasy

In the journey of embracing your fantasies, it is crucial to explore the depths of sensuality and fantasy. This subchapter is dedicated to helping sissy babies connect with their sensual desires and delve into the realms of fantasy. By understanding the power of sensuality and embracing your inner desires, you can unlock a world of pleasure and fulfillment.

Sensuality is a beautiful aspect of human existence that encompasses our senses, emotions, and physical experiences. It is the art of fully engaging with our bodies, minds, and surroundings to create a heightened state of pleasure and connection with ourselves and others. For sissy babies, sensuality holds immense potential for self-discovery and self-expression.

Through meditation and introspection, sissy babies can tap into their sensual desires and uncover the depths of their fantasies. By embracing sensuality, you can connect with your body, appreciate its beauty, and explore the sensations that bring you joy. This connection with your sensual self allows you to understand your desires, needs, and boundaries more deeply.

Fantasy, on the other hand, offers an escape from reality into a world of imagination and possibility. It is a safe haven where sissy babies can explore their deepest desires, uninhibited by societal norms or judgments. Understanding your fantasies allows you to create a roadmap for self-discovery and personal growth.

Meditations for sissy babies to connect with their sensual desires and fantasies provide a sacred space to explore and understand these aspects fully. Through guided visualization and self-reflection, you can allow yourself to freely explore your desires, no matter how unconventional they may seem. Embracing your fantasies is an empowering act that honors your true self and helps you cultivate a sense of authenticity and fulfillment.

Remember, sensuality and fantasy are deeply personal experiences. Each sissy baby's journey is unique, and there is no right or wrong way to embrace your desires. This subchapter aims to provide you with tools, guidance, and support as you navigate the intricate landscapes of sensuality and fantasy.

By embracing your sensuality and fantasies, you can embark on a transformative journey towards self-acceptance, self-love, and personal growth. So, take a deep breath, open your mind, and let the magic of sensuality and fantasy guide you towards a more fulfilling and authentic life as a sissy baby.

Defining Sensuality

Defining Sensuality: Exploring the Depths of Your Desires

In the journey of self-discovery, it is vital to embrace and understand our sensuality. For sissy babies, connecting with their sensual desires and fantasies can be a transformative experience, leading to a deeper understanding of themselves and the world around them. In this subchapter, we delve into the essence of sensuality and how it can positively impact your life.

Sensuality is often misunderstood, limited to mere physical pleasure. However, it encompasses so much more. It is the art of engaging all your senses, allowing yourself to revel in the beauty that surrounds you. It is about being present in the moment, fully immersed in the experience, and embracing the pleasures that lie within.

For sissy babies, sensuality can be a gateway to exploring their deepest desires and fantasies. It is a safe space where they can connect with their true selves, free from judgment or societal expectations. Through meditations, we can unlock the power of sensuality, liberating ourselves and embracing our unique journey.

Meditations for sissy babies to connect with their sensual desires and fantasies provide a sacred platform to explore and understand their innermost longings. By quieting the mind and focusing on the sensations that arise, one can tap into their innate sensuality, allowing it to guide them towards a more fulfilling life.

This subchapter will guide you through various meditative exercises designed to awaken your senses and explore your sensual fantasies. It will help you embrace the beauty of your desires, nurturing a deep connection with yourself and your fantasies.

By embracing your sensuality, you open the door to self-acceptance, self-love, and self-empowerment. You will discover the immense pleasure that lies within you, allowing your fantasies to weave seamlessly into your reality. Through meditations, you will learn to celebrate your uniqueness and cherish the sensual being you are.

In conclusion, defining sensuality is about exploring the depths of your desires and connecting with your sensual self. This subchapter serves as a guide for sissy babies to embrace their fantasies and connect with their sensuality through meditation. By embarking on this journey, you will uncover the true essence of who you are and find fulfillment in embracing your sensual desires.

The Power of Fantasy

In the intriguing world of sensuality, it is essential to acknowledge and embrace the power of fantasy. Fantasies hold a unique capability to transport us to realms beyond the confines of our ordinary lives, unlocking the depths of our desires and igniting our sensual selves. For sissy babies seeking to connect with their sensual desires, exploring the realm of fantasy can be a transformative and empowering journey.

Fantasies offer a safe space where sissy babies can explore their deepest passions, free from judgment or societal constraints. They allow us to delve into the uncharted territories of our imagination, where our sensual desires can bloom and flourish. Engaging in fantasies enables sissy babies to tap into their authentic selves, embracing their true sensuality without fear or hesitation.

Through fantasies, sissy babies can discover their unique identities and explore the various facets of their sensual desires. Whether it's indulging in the role of a seductive temptress, a submissive partner, or any other persona that resonates with their true self, fantasies open the doors to self-discovery and self-acceptance. They provide a platform for sissy babies to experiment with different roles and scenarios, enhancing their understanding of their sensual boundaries and preferences.

Moreover, fantasies have the extraordinary power to ignite passion and excitement within us. They can awaken dormant desires and kindle the flames of sensuality that may have been suppressed or overlooked. By embracing their fantasies, sissy babies can reclaim their personal power, allowing their desires to guide them on a path of self-expression and fulfillment.

Meditations specifically designed for sissy babies to connect with their sensual desires and fantasies can prove to be invaluable tools on this transformative journey. These meditations serve as gateways to access the deep recesses of the mind, where the seeds of fantasies lie dormant, waiting to be nourished and explored. By engaging in these meditations, sissy babies can cultivate a deeper connection with their fantasies, enabling them to tap into the wellspring of sensuality within.

In conclusion, the power of fantasy cannot be underestimated in the pursuit of sensual fulfillment for sissy babies. By embracing their fantasies and engaging in meditations tailored to their needs, sissy babies can embark on a transformative journey of self-discovery and self-acceptance. Through fantasies, they can explore their desires, fuel their passion, and ultimately embrace their true sensual selves. So, let your imagination run wild, dear sissy babies, and unlock the power of fantasy that lies within you.

Embracing Sensual Desires

In this subchapter, we will explore the beautiful world of sensuality and how sissy babies can connect with their deepest desires and fantasies. Sensuality is an integral part of our human experience, and embracing it can be a powerful tool for self-discovery and personal growth.

For sissy babies, sensuality takes on a unique form that allows them to explore their femininity and delve into their fantasies in a safe and empowering way. By embracing sensual desires, sissy babies can unlock a world of pleasure and self-expression, where their innermost fantasies can be acknowledged and celebrated.

Meditation is a powerful practice that can help sissy babies connect with their sensual desires on a deeper level. Through meditation, one can quiet the mind, cultivate self-awareness, and tap into the wellspring of their fantasies. By creating a sacred space and dedicating time to meditation, sissy babies can explore their sensual desires in a safe and non-judgmental environment.

During these meditations, sissy babies are encouraged to visualize and immerse themselves in their fantasies. Whether it's dressing up in exquisite lingerie, exploring role-play scenarios, or indulging in sensual activities, these meditations allow sissy babies to fully embrace their desires and experience them on a visceral level.

Furthermore, embracing sensual desires also involves accepting and loving oneself unconditionally. Sissy babies must recognize that their fantasies are a beautiful part of who they are and should be celebrated rather than repressed. By embracing their sensual desires, sissy babies can cultivate self-love, self-acceptance, and a deep sense of empowerment.

It is important to remember that embracing sensual desires is a personal journey, and each sissy baby will have their own unique fantasies and desires.

There is no right or wrong way to explore sensuality, as long as it is consensual, safe, and brings joy and fulfillment.

In conclusion, embracing sensual desires is a transformative journey for sissy babies to connect with their deepest fantasies and desires. Through the practice of meditation, sissy babies can tap into their sensual nature, embrace their femininity, and experience a profound sense of self-discovery and empowerment. By accepting and celebrating their desires, sissy babies can embark on a path of self-love, self-acceptance, and unbridled pleasure. So, let us embark on this journey together, embracing our sensuality and celebrating the beautiful fantasies that make us who we are.

Embracing Your Inner Sissy Baby

In the realm of sensuality and self-discovery, there exists a magical space where one can fully indulge in their deepest desires and fantasies. For those who identify as sissy babies, this journey of self-exploration holds an even more profound significance. "Embracing Your Fantasies: Meditations for Sissy Babies on Sensuality" is a transformative guide designed to help sissy babies connect with their sensual desires and uncover the true essence of their inner selves.

This subchapter, "Embracing Your Inner Sissy Baby," delves into the heart of what it means to fully embrace and celebrate one's sissy baby identity. It encourages sissy babies to shed societal expectations, judgments, and fears, and instead, revel in the pure bliss of their sensual desires and fantasies.

Through a series of meditative practices, this subchapter offers a safe and nurturing space for sissy babies to explore their innermost longings. It invites them to reconnect with their childlike innocence, vulnerability, and playfulness, allowing them to fully embrace their sissy baby identity without shame or guilt.

Within these pages, sissy babies will discover the power of self-acceptance and self-love. They will learn to honor their unique desires and fantasies as sacred expressions of their authentic selves. By embracing their inner sissy baby, they will unlock a world of pleasure, joy, and self-discovery that they may have previously feared or repressed.

Moreover, this subchapter provides practical advice on how sissy babies can incorporate their sensual desires into their daily lives. It offers guidance on creating safe spaces, building supportive communities, and communicating their needs and boundaries with partners and loved ones.

"Embracing Your Inner Sissy Baby" serves as a gentle reminder that every sissy baby is worthy of love, acceptance, and understanding. It encourages sissy babies to let go of any self-doubt or shame and embrace their authentic selves with open arms.

As you embark on this transformative journey, remember that your sensual desires and fantasies are beautiful and valid. Embrace your inner sissy baby, for it is within this embrace that you will discover the true essence of your being.

Understanding Sissy Baby Identity

In this subchapter, we will delve into the intricate world of sissy baby identity and explore the various aspects that contribute to the formation and expression of this unique persona. For sissy babies, embracing their fantasies and connecting with their sensual desires is a way to explore their innermost desires and find fulfillment in their lives.

Sissy baby identity encompasses a wide spectrum of emotions, desires, and fantasies. It is a personal journey that allows individuals to embrace their feminine side and find solace in expressing their sensual desires. It is important to note that sissy baby identity is not limited to gender or age; it transcends societal norms and provides a safe space for individuals to explore their fantasies.

One of the key elements in understanding sissy baby identity is self-acceptance. Sissy babies often struggle with societal expectations and judgments, which can lead to feelings of shame or guilt. However, by embracing their fantasies and desires, sissy babies can find a sense of liberation and self-empowerment. Through meditation and self-reflection, sissy babies can connect with their sensual desires and reconcile them with their everyday lives.

Meditation can be a powerful tool for sissy babies to explore their sensual desires and fantasies. By quieting the mind and focusing on their innermost desires, sissy babies can create a sacred space where they can fully embrace their fantasies without judgment or shame. Through guided meditations and visualizations, sissy babies can connect with their sensual energy and explore the depths of their desires.

Furthermore, understanding sissy baby identity involves exploring the emotional and psychological aspects of this persona. Sissy babies often find solace in the nurturing and caring aspects of their identity, which allows them to explore their sensual desires in a safe and consensual manner. By embracing their vulnerability and connecting with their sensual self, sissy babies can create a more fulfilling and authentic life.

In conclusion, understanding sissy baby identity is a personal journey that involves self-acceptance, meditation, and exploration of sensual desires and fantasies. By connecting with their innermost desires and embracing their vulnerability, sissy babies can find empowerment and fulfillment in their lives. Through meditations and self-reflection, sissy babies can create a sacred space where they can fully embrace their fantasies and connect with their sensual self. This subchapter aims to provide guidance and support for sissy babies on their journey of self-discovery and sensual exploration.

Embracing Your Sissy Baby Self

In the realm of sensuality, there exists a beautiful and diverse tapestry of desires and fantasies. Among these, the sissy baby community stands tall, offering a safe haven for those who yearn to explore their innermost sensual desires. This subchapter is dedicated to all the sissy babies out there, providing a gentle guide to help you embrace your true self and connect with your sensual fantasies on a deeper level.

To truly embrace your sissy baby self, it is crucial to first acknowledge and accept your desires without judgment. Understand that your fantasies are valid and deserve to be explored. This journey is about self-discovery and self-acceptance, allowing yourself to fully indulge in your sensual desires without shame or guilt.

Meditation can be a powerful tool in this process. Take the time to sit in a quiet space, allowing your mind to drift into a state of calm. Visualize yourself as the sissy baby you long to be, fully immersing yourself in the sensations and experiences that arouse your desires. Embrace the vulnerability and surrender to the pleasure that awaits you. Through meditation, you can tap into the depths of your sensual fantasies, connecting with them on a profound level.

Furthermore, explore the vast array of resources available to sissy babies. Online communities, forums, and support groups can provide a sense of belonging and understanding. Engage in conversations, share experiences, and learn from others who are on similar journeys. Remember, you are not alone in your desires, and there is strength in community.

As you embark on this journey of self-discovery, it is important to set boundaries and prioritize your safety. Consent and communication are key when exploring your fantasies with others. Seek out partners who understand and respect your desires, ensuring a consensual and mutually enjoyable experience.

Embracing your sissy baby self is a courageous act of self-love. It is a celebration of your unique sensuality and a testament to your willingness to explore the depths of your desires. By embracing your fantasies and connecting with your sensual side, you are opening the doors to a world of pleasure and self-acceptance.

Remember, dear sissy baby, you are deserving of love, pleasure, and happiness. Embrace your true self, indulge in your fantasies, and let your sensual desires guide you on a journey of self-discovery. Embrace the beauty of being a sissy baby, for it is through embracing our true selves that we find true liberation and fulfillment.

Overcoming Society's Stigma

Chapter 5: Overcoming Society's Stigma

In a world that often seeks to define and confine us within rigid gender norms, sissy babies face unique challenges when it comes to embracing their sensual desires and fantasies. Society's stigma can be suffocating, leaving many feeling ashamed and disconnected from their true selves. However, it is essential to recognize that the path to self-acceptance and liberation begins with overcoming this stigma.

Overcoming society's stigma requires a deep understanding and acceptance of oneself. It is crucial to remember that there is nothing wrong with embracing your fantasies and desires. They are an integral part of who you are and should be celebrated, rather than hidden away. Meditating on your sensual desires can help you connect with your authentic self, allowing you to break free from societal constraints.

One powerful technique to overcome society's stigma is by challenging the limiting beliefs that have been imposed upon you. Recognize that these beliefs are not your own but rather a product of societal conditioning. By questioning and reframing these beliefs, you can create a new narrative that empowers and celebrates your sensual desires.

It is also important to surround yourself with a supportive community. Seek out like-minded individuals who understand and embrace their own sensuality. Connecting with others who share similar experiences can provide a sense of validation and belonging. Online forums, support groups, and even local meetups can be excellent resources for finding such communities.

Additionally, practicing self-compassion is vital in overcoming society's stigma. Be gentle with yourself and understand that it is okay to experience moments of doubt or insecurity. Embrace your vulnerabilities, knowing that they are a part of your journey towards self-acceptance. Treat yourself with kindness and love, just as you would a close friend.

Remember, overcoming society's stigma is a process, and it may take time. But by embracing your fantasies and connecting with your sensual desires, you are reclaiming your power and embracing your true self. You are breaking free from the chains of societal expectations and forging your own path towards self-fulfillment and happiness.

Embrace your sensuality, sissy babies, and know that you deserve to live a life filled with joy, authenticity, and pleasure. By taking these steps, you are not only empowering yourself but also paving the way for others to do the same. Society's stigma may be strong, but your inner strength and determination are even stronger.

Chapter 2: Creating a Safe Space for Sensual Exploration

Establishing Boundaries

In the journey of exploring our sensuality and embracing our fantasies, it is crucial for sissy babies to establish clear boundaries. Boundaries serve as a protective framework that allows us to feel safe, respected, and in control of our desires. By setting and maintaining these boundaries, we can create a space where we can fully immerse ourselves in our sensual exploration without fear or judgment.

Boundaries can manifest in various forms, including physical, emotional, and psychological boundaries. Let's delve into each aspect and understand how they contribute to our growth as sissy babies.

Physical boundaries involve defining what is acceptable and comfortable in terms of touch, proximity, and personal space. As sissy babies, it is important to communicate our physical boundaries clearly to our partners or playmates. This can include specifying which body parts are off-limits, setting limits on the intensity of physical interaction, or establishing a safe word to signal when we feel overwhelmed or uncomfortable.

Emotional boundaries pertain to our emotional well-being and ensuring that we are not subjected to emotional manipulation or coercion. As sissy babies, it is our responsibility to communicate our emotional needs and limitations to our partners or playmates. This includes expressing our feelings, desires, and any emotional triggers that may arise during our sensual explorations.

Psychological boundaries involve establishing limits on the types of fantasies or role-playing scenarios we are comfortable with. As sissy babies, it is important to be honest with ourselves and our partners about our boundaries regarding specific fantasies or fetishes. By setting these limits, we can ensure that our sensual experiences align with our desires and comfort levels.

Establishing boundaries is an ongoing process that requires self-reflection, communication, and self-advocacy. It is essential for sissy babies to regularly check in with themselves and assess whether their boundaries are being respected and honored. Remember, it is perfectly acceptable to modify or adjust boundaries as we grow and evolve in our sensual journey.

In conclusion, establishing boundaries is a vital aspect of embracing our fantasies and connecting with our sensual desires as sissy babies. By clearly defining our physical, emotional, and psychological limits, we create a safe and empowering space for our sensual exploration. Remember, boundaries are not limitations but rather tools for self-care and self-expression. Embrace your boundaries with confidence, communicate them effectively, and enjoy the transformative power of connecting with your sensuality.

Setting Personal Boundaries

In the journey of embracing your fantasies and connecting with your sensual desires as a sissy baby, setting personal boundaries becomes an essential aspect of self-care and self-discovery. Understanding and asserting your boundaries is crucial to ensure your emotional and physical well-being. This subchapter aims to guide you through the process of establishing and maintaining healthy personal boundaries, allowing you to explore your sensuality in a safe and empowering way.

Firstly, it is important to acknowledge that your desires and fantasies are unique and deserve respect. Embracing your sensuality should be a consensual and enjoyable experience for you. By setting personal boundaries, you create a framework that safeguards your emotional and physical comfort while exploring your fantasies.

Start by reflecting on your needs and desires. What are your hard limits? What activities or situations make you uncomfortable or feel unsafe? Identifying these boundaries empowers you to communicate them effectively with others, ensuring your boundaries are respected.

Once you have identified your boundaries, it is crucial to communicate them assertively and clearly. Remember, your boundaries are valid, and you have the right to express them. Practice using "I" statements to communicate your limits, such as "I am not comfortable with..." or "I need to set a boundary around...". This approach encourages open and respectful dialogue with your partners or playmates, fostering an environment of trust and consent.

Boundaries are not fixed; they may evolve as you explore your sensuality further. Regularly reassessing and adjusting your boundaries is key to maintaining a healthy and fulfilling journey. Take time to reflect on your experiences and emotions, and be willing to communicate any changes in your boundaries to those involved. Remember, your boundaries should always align with your comfort and well-being.

Furthermore, it is essential to surround yourself with individuals who respect and support your boundaries. Establishing a supportive network of like-minded individuals or joining communities where you can openly discuss your desires can provide a safe space for exploration and growth. Connecting with others who share similar experiences can also help you navigate challenges and learn from their insights.

In conclusion, setting personal boundaries is a vital aspect of embracing your fantasies and connecting with your sensual desires as a sissy baby. By recognizing and communicating your limits, you create a safe and empowering environment for exploration. Regularly reassessing and adjusting your boundaries, as well as surrounding yourself with supportive individuals, will enhance your journey of self-discovery, ensuring it remains a consensual, enjoyable, and fulfilling experience.

Communicating Boundaries with Partners

In the thrilling journey of embracing your sensuality, it is crucial to learn how to communicate your boundaries effectively with your partners. As sissy babies, exploring your desires and fantasies requires a delicate balance of vulnerability and assertiveness. This subchapter will guide you through the art of setting boundaries, ensuring that your sensual experiences are safe, consensual, and fulfilling.

Understanding your own boundaries is the first step towards fostering healthy and enjoyable connections with your partners. Take the time to reflect on your desires, limits, and comfort zones. Remember, your boundaries are valid and deserve to be honored. Embrace your authentic self and be unapologetic about your needs.

Once you have a clear understanding of your boundaries, it is essential to communicate them openly and honestly with your partner(s). Effective communication promotes trust, respect, and mutual understanding. Share your desires, limits, and fantasies, allowing your partner(s) to understand your needs fully. Expressing your boundaries can be liberating, as it ensures that your sensual experiences align with your desires.

When communicating boundaries, it is crucial to use assertive language. Be confident and firm in expressing your limits and desires. Remember, your boundaries are not up for negotiation. If your partner(s) respect and care for you, they will honor your boundaries without question. If anyone tries to pressure or coerce you into crossing your limits, it is a clear sign of a lack of respect and consent. In such cases, it is important to reassess the relationship and consider seeking support from trusted friends or professionals.

Additionally, listening to and respecting your partner(s)' boundaries is equally vital. Consent is a two-way street, and everyone's boundaries deserve to be acknowledged. Create a safe space for open dialogue, where both you and your partner(s) feel comfortable expressing your limits and desires. By fostering a culture of consent and respect, you can build deeper connections and ensure that your sensual experiences are enjoyable and fulfilling for all parties involved.

In conclusion, mastering the art of communicating boundaries is an essential skill for sissy babies on their sensual journey. By understanding and asserting your boundaries, you can create a safe and consensual space for exploring your desires and fantasies. Remember, your boundaries are valid, and they deserve to be respected. Embrace your sensuality with confidence, and let your desires guide you towards blissful fulfillment.

Respecting Others' Boundaries

In the journey of embracing your sensual desires and fantasies as a sissy baby, it is crucial to understand and respect the boundaries of others. Just as you seek a safe and accepting space to explore your sensuality, it is equally important to honor the limits and comfort zones of those around you.

Respecting others' boundaries is not only a sign of empathy and maturity but also a way to build trust and maintain healthy relationships. It allows for open communication and ensures that all parties involved feel safe and respected in their interactions.

As a sissy baby, it is essential to remember that not everyone shares the same desires or fantasies as you. Each person has their own unique interests, limits, and comfort levels. It is crucial to approach others with understanding and respect, seeking their consent before engaging in any activities or discussions that may involve crossing personal boundaries.

Consent is the cornerstone of respecting others' boundaries. Always obtain explicit and enthusiastic consent before engaging in any sensual or intimate activities with another person. This includes both physical and emotional boundaries. Remember, no means no, and consent can be withdrawn at any time.

Listening actively is another integral part of respecting others' boundaries. Pay attention to verbal and non-verbal cues that indicate discomfort or disinterest. Be attuned to the needs and limits of others and be willing to adjust your behavior accordingly.

Boundaries are not limitations; they are essential for personal growth and self-care. By respecting others' boundaries, you are creating a positive and inclusive environment for everyone involved. It allows individuals to feel comfortable expressing themselves without fear of judgment or intrusion.

In your meditations as a sissy baby, take time to reflect on the importance of respecting others' boundaries. Consider how your actions and desires impact those around you. Cultivate an attitude of empathy, understanding, and unconditional acceptance.

Remember, embracing your fantasies is a personal journey, but it should never come at the expense of others. By establishing and respecting boundaries, you can create a harmonious and consensual space for exploration, growth, and connection with your sensual desires as a sissy baby.

Building a Supportive Community

In the enchanting journey of embracing your fantasies and connecting with your sensual desires as a sissy baby, building a supportive community is vital. This subchapter delves into the transformative power of surrounding yourself with like-minded individuals who understand and celebrate your unique journey.

As a sissy baby, it is crucial to find a safe space where you can freely express your desires and explore your sensuality without fear of judgment or ridicule. This supportive community becomes your sanctuary, a place where you can be your authentic self without any pretenses. Here, you will find solace and understanding, knowing that you are not alone on this extraordinary path.

When seeking a supportive community, it is essential to find individuals who share similar interests and experiences. Engaging with fellow sissy babies who are also on a quest for self-discovery and sensual fulfillment can be incredibly empowering. By connecting with others who understand your desires, you create a network of support, validation, and guidance.

Within this community, you will find a wealth of knowledge and wisdom. Through shared experiences and conversations, you can learn from others' journeys, gaining insights and inspiration to further explore your own sensual fantasies. As you engage in meditations designed specifically for sissy babies, you will discover new dimensions of pleasure and fulfillment that you may have never imagined.

Additionally, building a supportive community allows for the exchange of ideas and resources. From recommendations for books, films, and artwork to suggestions for workshops or events, your community becomes a wellspring of inspiration. By sharing these resources, you empower each other to continue expanding your sensual horizons and embracing your deepest desires.

Remember, building a supportive community is a two-way street. Just as you seek understanding and acceptance, be prepared to offer the same to others. Embrace the diversity within your community, acknowledging that everyone's journey is unique and equally valid. By fostering a non-judgmental and inclusive environment, you create a space where everyone can flourish and grow.

In conclusion, building a supportive community is an essential aspect of your journey as a sissy baby. By connecting with like-minded individuals, you create a sanctuary where you can freely explore your sensual desires and fantasies. This community becomes a source of support, validation, and inspiration, allowing you to embrace your fantasies with confidence and grace. Together, you and your community can embark on a transformative journey of self-discovery and sensual fulfillment.

Finding Like-Minded Individuals

In the journey of embracing your fantasies and connecting with your sensual desires as a sissy baby, it is crucial to surround yourself with like-minded individuals who understand and support you. These individuals can provide the validation, acceptance, and guidance you need to fully explore and express your true self. However, finding such companions can be a challenge in a world where societal norms often stifle unconventional desires. This subchapter aims to offer insights and practical tips on how to discover and connect with like-minded individuals who share your meditations for sissy babies to connect with their sensual desires and fantasies.

Firstly, it is important to remember that you are not alone. The online world provides a vast network of communities, forums, and social media groups dedicated to exploring alternative lifestyles and sensual desires. Engaging with these platforms can open doors to meeting fellow sissy babies who are on a similar journey. These digital spaces allow for anonymity, which can help you feel more comfortable when sharing your fantasies and desires.

Seeking out local events, workshops, or conventions that cater to the sissy baby community can also be an excellent way to meet like-minded individuals in person. These gatherings often provide safe spaces for individuals to express themselves without judgment. Attending such events can be a transformative experience, allowing you to connect with others who share similar meditations and desires.

Another method to find like-minded individuals is through professional guidance. Seeking the support of a therapist, counselor, or coach who specializes in alternative lifestyles can help you navigate your journey and connect with a community of like-minded individuals. These professionals can provide invaluable insights, support, and resources that are specifically tailored to your needs.

Remember, finding like-minded individuals may require some patience and perseverance. It is essential to approach it with an open mind and an open heart. Building connections takes time, so be patient with yourself and others. Taking small steps to engage with the community, whether online or in-person, can gradually lead to meaningful relationships that will enrich your journey of embracing your fantasies and connecting with your sensual desires as a sissy baby.

In conclusion, finding like-minded individuals is an integral part of your journey towards self-discovery and acceptance as a sissy baby. By exploring online platforms, attending local events, seeking professional guidance, and being patient with the process, you can connect with individuals who share your meditations for sissy babies to connect with their sensual desires and fantasies. Remember that you deserve understanding, validation, and support, and by seeking out like-minded individuals, you are taking a significant step towards embracing your true self.

Online Communities for Sissy Babies

In this modern age of technology, the internet has become a vast landscape of possibilities, connecting people from all walks of life. For sissy babies, this digital realm offers a unique opportunity to explore and embrace their sensual desires and fantasies. Online communities dedicated to sissy babies have emerged as safe spaces for individuals to connect, share experiences, and find support on their journey towards self-discovery.

These online communities provide a platform for sissy babies to connect with like-minded individuals who understand and appreciate their unique desires. Within these virtual spaces, sissy babies can freely express themselves, discuss their fantasies, and seek guidance from others who have walked a similar path. This sense of belonging fosters a supportive and non-judgmental environment, allowing sissy babies to explore their sensual side without fear of rejection or ridicule.

One of the key benefits of these online communities is the opportunity for sissy babies to engage in meditative practices. Through various guided meditations, individuals are encouraged to connect with their sensual desires on a deeper level, allowing them to explore the intricacies of their fantasies. These meditations provide a safe and nurturing space for sissy babies to embrace their fantasies and understand the emotional and psychological aspects behind their desires.

Within these communities, sissy babies can also find a wealth of resources to further enhance their sensual experiences. From recommended reading materials to workshops and events, these online platforms become a treasure trove of knowledge and inspiration. Sissy babies can delve into the world of sensuality, discovering new techniques, exploring different role-playing scenarios, and expanding their understanding of their desires.

It is important to note that while these online communities provide a valuable space for sissy babies to explore their sensuality, caution must be exercised. It is crucial to prioritize safety and consent in all interactions. Engaging in open and honest communication, setting boundaries, and respecting the boundaries of others is essential to maintaining a healthy and respectful online community.

In conclusion, online communities for sissy babies offer a unique and empowering platform for self-discovery and exploration of sensuality. These spaces provide support, guidance, and a sense of belonging for sissy babies who wish to connect with their deepest desires and fantasies. Through guided meditations and access to valuable resources, individuals can embark on a transformative journey towards embracing their fantasies and living a more fulfilling life.

Creating Local Support Groups

In the journey of embracing your fantasies and connecting with your sensual desires as a sissy baby, having a strong support system is crucial. Local support groups can offer a safe and understanding space where you can freely express yourself, share experiences, and seek guidance from like-minded individuals who are also exploring their sensuality.

One of the first steps in creating a local support group for sissy babies is to find potential members. This can be done through online communities, forums, or even reaching out to local fetish clubs or adult stores that may have connections to the sissy baby community. Remember, discretion and respect for privacy are paramount, so ensure that all potential members are comfortable with joining a support group and that their identities will be protected.

Once you have gathered a small group of individuals interested in joining the local support group, it is essential to establish clear guidelines and boundaries to ensure a safe and respectful environment. Determine the purpose of the group, whether it is for sharing experiences, offering emotional support, or organizing social gatherings. Setting these guidelines from the beginning will help create a sense of trust and clarity among the members.

Regular meetings should be organized to foster connection and provide a platform for open discussions. These meetings can take various formats, such as casual coffee meet-ups, structured sharing circles, or even educational workshops led by experts in relevant fields. By offering a range of activities, you can cater to the diverse needs and interests of the group members, ensuring that everyone feels included and supported.

In addition to regular meetings, consider organizing social events or outings that allow the group to bond and explore their sensual desires in a safe and non-judgmental environment. These events could include themed parties, outings to fetish clubs, or even weekend retreats focused on self-exploration and personal growth.

Creating a local support group for sissy babies is an empowering way to connect with others who share similar desires and fantasies. By fostering a supportive and inclusive community, you can embark on a journey of self-discovery, self-acceptance, and self-love. Remember, it is essential to respect each other's boundaries, maintain confidentiality, and create a non-judgmental space where individuals can freely express themselves. Embrace your fantasies and let the local support group be your guiding light on this sensual journey.

Chapter 3: Meditation Practices for Sensual Connection

Mindfulness Meditation

Mindfulness Meditation: Embracing Sensuality and Fantasies

In this subchapter, we will explore the transformative power of mindfulness meditation for sissy babies to connect with their sensual desires and fantasies. Mindfulness meditation is a practice that allows individuals to cultivate a deep sense of awareness and presence in the present moment. It can be a powerful tool for sissy babies to explore and embrace their unique sensualities in a safe and non-judgmental space.

For sissy babies, sensuality and fantasies are often intertwined with their identity and self-expression. Through mindfulness meditation, you can learn to observe your thoughts, emotions, and sensations without judgment or attachment. This practice enables you to become more attuned to your desires and fantasies, allowing you to explore and embrace them in a healthy and fulfilling way.

To begin your mindfulness meditation practice, find a quiet and comfortable space where you can sit or lie down. Close your eyes and take a few deep breaths, allowing your body and mind to relax. As you settle into this moment, bring your attention to your breath, feeling the sensation of each inhale and exhale.

As you continue to breathe, allow your mind to wander and explore your sensual desires and fantasies. Notice any thoughts or images that arise without judgment or resistance. Instead of pushing them away, embrace them with curiosity and compassion. Remember, this is a safe space for you to explore and honor your unique desires.

While engaging in mindfulness meditation, you may encounter moments of discomfort or resistance. This is natural, as exploring sensuality and fantasies can sometimes challenge societal norms or personal beliefs. As you encounter these moments, remind yourself that your desires are valid and deserving of acceptance.

As your mindfulness practice deepens, you will develop a greater sense of self-awareness and acceptance, leading to a more profound connection with your sensual desires and fantasies. Remember to approach this journey with kindness and patience, knowing that it is an ongoing process of self-discovery and self-acceptance.

In conclusion, mindfulness meditation is a powerful practice for sissy babies to connect with their sensual desires and fantasies. By embracing mindfulness, you can create a safe and non-judgmental space to explore and honor your unique self-expression. Embrace your fantasies, sissy babies, and let mindfulness meditation guide you on a transformative journey towards self-acceptance and fulfillment.

Techniques for Focusing the Mind

Title: Techniques for Focusing the Mind: Embracing Sensuality for Sissy Babies

Introduction:
In this subchapter, we will explore techniques specifically designed to help sissy babies embrace their sensuality and connect with their deepest desires and fantasies. By learning to focus the mind, sissy babies can create a safe and nurturing space to explore their sensual nature and fully embrace their fantasies. These techniques will enable you to build a strong foundation for personal growth, self-acceptance, and the discovery of your true sensual self.

1. Mindful Breathing:
Begin by finding a quiet space where you can be alone. Close your eyes and

take a deep breath, allowing the air to fill your lungs. As you exhale, release any tension or negative thoughts. Focus your attention on the sensation of your breath, feeling it move in and out of your body. This practice of mindful breathing helps to calm the mind and brings you into the present moment, allowing you to connect with your sensual desires.

2. Visualization:

Using the power of your imagination, visualize yourself in a safe and comfortable environment where you can freely express your sensuality. Create a mental picture of the surroundings, the scents, and the sounds that bring you pleasure. This visualization technique allows sissy babies to tap into their fantasies and helps to build confidence in embracing their sensual side.

3. Sensory Exploration:

Engage your senses to deepen your connection with your sensual fantasies. Experiment with various textures, scents, and tastes that evoke pleasure and excitement. Whether it's indulging in a luxurious bubble bath, wearing soft satin lingerie, or savoring a delicious treat, allow yourself to fully immerse in the sensory experience. By doing so, you are embracing your desires and cultivating a stronger connection with your sensual self.

4. Affirmations:

Create positive affirmations that resonate with your sensual desires and fantasies. Repeat these affirmations daily, either silently or out loud, to reinforce your belief in your sensual nature. For example, you could say, "I am worthy of embracing my fantasies and exploring my sensual desires." By affirming these beliefs, you are empowering yourself to fully embrace your sensuality.

Conclusion:

By incorporating these techniques into your daily practice, you will be able to focus your mind and create a safe space to connect with your sensuality as a sissy baby. Remember, it is essential to approach these practices with self-acceptance, love, and respect. Embracing your fantasies and desires is a personal journey, and by dedicating time to cultivate your sensual nature, you are honoring your authentic self.

Cultivating Awareness of Sensual Desires

In the journey of embracing your fantasies and exploring your sensuality, it is essential to cultivate an awareness of your sensual desires. As sissy babies, you may have unique inclinations and interests that can be explored and understood through meditation and self-reflection.

Meditation is a powerful tool that allows you to connect with your innermost desires and fantasies. By creating a safe and nurturing space, you can delve into the depths of your consciousness, exploring the sensual landscape that lies within. Through meditation, you can cultivate a heightened awareness of your sensual desires, enabling you to embrace them fully and without judgment.

During your meditative practice, it is important to approach your sensual desires with curiosity and openness. Allow yourself to explore the various facets of your fantasies, understanding that they are an integral part of your identity and should be embraced. Rather than suppressing or denying these desires, meditation encourages you to accept and celebrate them.

As you connect with your sensual desires through meditation, you may find it helpful to visualize yourself in various scenarios or engage in guided imagery. This allows you to fully immerse yourself in the sensations and emotions associated with your fantasies. By doing so, you can tap into the depths of your sensuality, experiencing pleasure and fulfillment on a profound level.

Remember that your sensual desires are unique to you, and they should be respected and cherished. By cultivating awareness of these desires, you can gain a deeper understanding of your authentic self and cultivate a sense of self-acceptance. Embracing your fantasies is not about conforming to societal norms but rather honoring your true desires and finding joy in expressing them.

Through meditation, you can develop a stronger connection with your sensual desires, allowing them to guide you on your journey of self-discovery and fulfillment. As sissy babies, meditations that focus on connecting with your sensuality can provide a transformative and empowering experience, helping you embrace your fantasies with confidence and authenticity.

In conclusion, cultivating awareness of your sensual desires through meditation is a powerful way to connect with your authentic self. By exploring your fantasies and embracing them without judgment, you can unlock a world of pleasure and self-acceptance. Through this practice, you can embark on a journey of self-discovery, finding joy and fulfillment in expressing your unique sensuality as a sissy baby.

Incorporating Sensual Imagery

Incorporating Sensual Imagery: Embrace Your Fantasies and Connect with Your Sensual Desires

Welcome, sissy babies, to this empowering subchapter titled "Incorporating Sensual Imagery" from our book, "Embracing Your Fantasies: Meditations for Sissy Babies on Sensuality." Here, we delve into the realm of your sensuality, helping you explore and connect with your deepest desires and fantasies.

As sissy babies, you possess a unique and beautiful perspective on sensuality. It is essential to understand that embracing your fantasies is not only acceptable but also encouraged. By doing so, you can experience a profound sense of self-discovery and empowerment.

In this subchapter, we will guide you through the process of incorporating sensual imagery into your meditative practices. Sensual imagery allows you to create a vivid mental landscape, where you can explore and indulge in your most intimate desires. It acts as a catalyst, stimulating your senses and awakening your sensuality on a profound level.

To begin, find a quiet and comfortable space where you can fully immerse yourself in this practice. Close your eyes and take a deep breath, allowing your mind to calm and your body to relax. Visualize a serene environment, such as a lush garden or a secluded beach, where you feel safe and free to explore.

Now, slowly introduce sensual imagery into your visualization. Picture yourself adorned in exquisite lingerie, feeling the delicate fabric against your skin. Imagine the soft touch of feathers, the scent of scented candles, or the taste of succulent strawberries. Let these images ignite your senses and awaken your sensuality.

As you continue your meditation, allow yourself to delve deeper into your fantasies. Embrace the role-playing scenarios that excite you, such as being pampered by a dominant partner or exploring your feminine side in a safe and supportive environment. Let go of any inhibitions and fully immerse yourself in these fantasies, knowing that they are an integral part of your journey.

Remember, sissy babies, that this journey is about self-discovery and self-acceptance. Embrace your sensual desires and fantasies without judgment. By incorporating sensual imagery into your meditative practices, you will connect with your truest self, fostering a deeper understanding of your sensuality and unlocking a world of pleasure and empowerment.

As you conclude your meditation, take a moment to appreciate the growth and self-awareness you have achieved. Know that you are on a beautiful path towards embracing your fantasies and connecting with your sensuality. Embrace your desires, sissy babies, and let them guide you towards a life of fulfillment and joy.

Breathwork and Sensuality

Subchapter: Breathwork and Sensuality

Welcome, dear Sissy Babies, to this transformative subchapter on breathwork and sensuality. In the realm of embracing your fantasies and connecting with your sensual desires, the power of breath is a tool that can take you on an incredible journey of self-discovery and fulfillment.

Breathwork is a practice that involves conscious, intentional breathing techniques to promote relaxation, stimulate energy flow, and enhance overall well-being. When combined with sensuality, it becomes a gateway to exploring the depths of your desires and fantasies, allowing you to connect with your innermost self on a profound level.

As Sissy Babies, you may have already discovered the immense pleasure and liberation in embracing your sensual side. This journey is about embracing your fantasies and becoming more in tune with your desires, allowing yourself the freedom to explore and express your true self.

Through breathwork, you can tap into the power of your breath as a vehicle for unlocking hidden depths of sensuality within you. The breath becomes a bridge that connects your mind, body, and spirit, facilitating a deep sense of self-awareness and presence in the moment.

By consciously focusing on your breath, you can release any inhibitions or limitations that may be holding you back from fully embracing your fantasies. As you inhale, imagine drawing in the essence of sensuality and desire, allowing it to flow through every cell of your being. With each exhale, let go of any negative self-judgment or shame that may hinder your exploration.

Breathwork can also be a powerful tool for intensifying pleasure and deepening connection during sensual experiences. By using specific breathing techniques, you can heighten your awareness of sensation and amplify the pleasure you derive from your fantasies.

As you continue to practice breathwork and explore your sensuality, remember to approach it with love, acceptance, and compassion for yourself. Embrace your fantasies as a beautiful and integral part of who you are, allowing yourself to experience the full range of pleasure and satisfaction they offer.

In conclusion, dear Sissy Babies, breathwork and sensuality go hand in hand on the path of self-discovery and embracing your fantasies. Through conscious breathing techniques, you can unlock the depths of your desires, intensify pleasure, and connect with your sensual self on a profound level. Embrace the power of breath and allow it to guide you on an extraordinary journey of self-exploration and fulfillment.

Deep Breathing Exercises

In this subchapter, we will explore the incredible power of deep breathing exercises and how they can help sissy babies connect with their sensual desires and fantasies. Breathing is a fundamental and often overlooked aspect of our existence, yet it holds immense potential for enhancing our sensual experiences.

For sissy babies seeking to explore their sensuality, deep breathing exercises offer a gateway to a world of self-discovery and self-acceptance. By consciously focusing on our breath, we can cultivate a deeper connection with our bodies and tap into the wellspring of our desires.

One powerful technique is called the "Square Breath." Begin by finding a comfortable position, whether sitting or lying down. Close your eyes and bring your attention to your breath. Inhale deeply through your nose, counting to four. Hold your breath for another count of four. Exhale slowly through your mouth, again counting to four. Finally, hold your breath for another count of four before repeating the cycle. As you practice this exercise, visualize yourself embracing your sensual desires and fantasies, allowing them to flow freely throughout your being.

Another effective method is the "Ocean Breath." Imagine yourself sitting on a secluded beach, with the rhythmic sound of waves crashing against the shore.

Inhale slowly and deeply through your nose, imagining the cool ocean breeze filling your lungs. As you exhale, let out a long, gentle sigh, mimicking the sound of the waves receding back into the vast expanse of the ocean. With each breath, allow yourself to surrender to the sensuality that resides within you.

Deep breathing exercises can also be combined with affirmations and visualizations. As you inhale, repeat affirmations such as "I embrace my sensuality" or "I am worthy of exploring my fantasies." As you exhale, visualize yourself shedding any inhibitions or doubts, allowing your desires to take flight.

Remember, sissy babies, that deep breathing exercises are a powerful tool for connecting with your sensual desires and fantasies. Practice them regularly, dedicating time and space to explore your sensuality without judgment or shame. Embrace the transformative potential of your breath and embark on a journey of self-discovery, acceptance, and pleasure.

In the next subchapter, we will delve deeper into the art of visualization and how it can enhance your sensual experiences. Stay tuned and continue embracing your fantasies!

Connecting Breath and Sensual Energy

In the world of sensuality and fantasies, there is a powerful tool that often goes unnoticed – our breath. The simple act of breathing has the potential to awaken our sensual energy and connect us with our deepest desires. For sissy babies seeking to explore their sensual side, understanding and harnessing the power of their breath can be a transformative experience.

Breath is the life force that flows through our bodies, connecting us to the present moment and allowing us to tap into our sensual desires. By focusing on our breath, we can cultivate a sense of mindfulness and awareness, which is essential for embracing our fantasies.

To begin the journey of connecting breath and sensual energy, find a quiet and comfortable space where you can fully relax. Take a moment to close your eyes and bring your attention to your breath. Notice the sensation of the air entering and leaving your body, the rise and fall of your chest, and the rhythm of your inhales and exhales.

As you become aware of your breath, let it guide you deeper into your body. With each inhalation, imagine drawing in sensual energy, filling every cell of your being with desire and pleasure. As you exhale, release any tension or inhibitions that may be holding you back from fully embracing your fantasies.

Experiment with different breathing techniques to enhance your sensual experience. Try slow, deep breaths to create a sense of calm and relaxation, or explore quick, shallow breaths to ignite a feeling of anticipation and excitement. Allow your breath to guide you on a journey of self-discovery and exploration.

As you connect with your breath and sensual energy, don't be afraid to let your fantasies come to life. Embrace the unique desires and fantasies that make you who you are, without judgment or shame. Allow your breath to be a conduit for your sensual energy, guiding you deeper into a world of pleasure and self-discovery.

Remember, connecting breath and sensual energy is a practice that requires patience and self-compassion. Be gentle with yourself as you explore this powerful connection, and always listen to your body's needs and boundaries.

By embracing the power of your breath and connecting with your sensual energy, you can unlock a world of pleasure and fulfillment. Through meditation and self-exploration, sissy babies can connect with their deepest desires and fantasies, creating a path towards self-acceptance and empowerment. So take a deep breath and embark on this transformative journey of connecting breath and sensual energy.

Awakening Sensual Desires through Breathwork

In the magical realm of sensuality, there exists a profound connection between our breath and our deepest desires. By harnessing the power of breathwork, sissy babies can embark on a transformative journey that will awaken their sensual desires and fantasies like never before.

Breathing is an instinctive action that sustains our lives, but it can also serve as a gateway to unlocking our hidden sensuality. Through intentional, conscious breathing exercises, sissy babies can tap into their sensual energy and explore the depths of their fantasies.

The first step in this journey is to find a quiet and comfortable space where you can fully immerse yourself in the practice of breathwork. Sit or lie down in a position that allows your body to relax completely, and close your eyes to shut out any external distractions. Take a moment to center yourself and set an intention to connect with your sensual desires.

Begin by taking slow, deep breaths, inhaling through your nose and exhaling through your mouth. As you breathe in, imagine that you are drawing in the essence of sensuality, filling your entire being with its intoxicating energy. With each exhale, release any tension or resistance that may be holding you back from fully embracing your fantasies.

As you continue to breathe deeply, allow your mind to wander and explore the depths of your sensual desires. Visualize yourself in the scenarios that ignite your fantasies, feeling the emotions and sensations as if they were real. Let go of any judgment or shame that may arise and fully embrace the freedom to explore your desires.

The power of breathwork lies in its ability to awaken our senses and connect us with our deepest desires. Through this practice, sissy babies can cultivate a greater sense of self-awareness, acceptance, and empowerment. By exploring their sensuality through breathwork, they can tap into a wellspring of pleasure and fulfillment that exists within them.

Remember, dear sissy babies, that your sensual desires are valid and beautiful. Embrace them fully and use breathwork as a tool to connect with the essence of your fantasies. Allow yourself the freedom to explore and indulge in the richness of your sensuality, knowing that it is a sacred part of who you are.

In the realm of sensuality, breathwork is the key that unlocks the door to a world of pleasure and self-discovery. Take a deep breath, dear sissy babies, and let your desires guide you on this exquisite journey of awakening.

Tantric Gazing Meditations

Subchapter: Tantric Gazing Meditations

Welcome, dear Sissy Babies, to the enchanting world of tantric gazing meditations. In this subchapter, we will explore a profound practice that will help you connect with your sensual desires and fantasies on a deep, spiritual level. By embracing these meditations, you will embark on a journey of self-discovery, love, and acceptance.

Tantric gazing meditations are rooted in the ancient practice of Tantra, a philosophy that celebrates sensuality and embraces pleasure as a pathway to spiritual enlightenment. This practice invites you to explore the power of your gaze as a means of connecting with your innermost desires.

In these meditations, you will learn to focus your gaze on objects, images, or even your own reflection. Through the art of gazing, you will begin to tap into the depths of your sensuality, allowing your fantasies to unfold before your eyes.

As you embark on this journey, it is essential to create a safe and sacred space for your practice. Find a quiet corner of your home, adorn it with soft, sensual fabrics, and create an atmosphere that reflects your desires. Light candles, play soft music, and surround yourself with items that evoke feelings of sensuality and femininity.

To begin your tantric gazing meditation, find a comfortable position and take a few deep breaths, centering yourself in the present moment. Allow your eyes to soften as you focus your gaze on the chosen object or image. As you continue to gaze, let your mind wander and explore the depths of your fantasies. Embrace the sensations that arise within you, without judgment or shame.

Through these meditations, you will learn to embrace your fantasies as a valid and beautiful part of your being. By connecting with your sensual desires, you will develop a deeper understanding of yourself and the power of your femininity. Remember, dear Sissy Babies, that your fantasies are sacred and deserving of love and acceptance.

As you conclude your tantric gazing meditation, take a moment to reflect on the sensations and emotions that arose during your practice. Journal your experiences, allowing them to unfold on the pages before you. By acknowledging and embracing your fantasies, you are nurturing your soul and honoring the essence of who you truly are.

Embrace the power of tantric gazing meditations, dear Sissy Babies, and unlock the doors to your sensual desires and fantasies. Through this practice, you will discover a world of self-love, acceptance, and profound connection with your truest, most authentic self.

Chakra Bonding Meditations

Title: Chakra Bonding Meditations: Embracing Sensuality for Sissy Babies

Introduction:
In this subchapter, we delve into the world of Chakra Bonding Meditations,

providing sissy babies with a transformative journey towards connecting with their sensual desires and fantasies. By exploring the intricate energy centers within our bodies, known as chakras, we aim to help sissy babies embrace their inner selves and unlock their sensuality in a safe and nurturing environment.

Understanding Chakras and Sensuality:
Chakras are powerful energy centers that exist within each of us, governing various aspects of our physical, emotional, and spiritual well-being. By working with these chakras, sissy babies can tap into their sensuality, uncovering hidden desires and fantasies, and allowing themselves to freely express their true selves.

Exploring Chakra Bonding Meditations:
1. Root Chakra: Grounding and Stability
Begin your journey by connecting with your root chakra, located at the base of your spine. Visualize a vibrant red light enveloping this energy center, grounding you to the Earth and giving you a sense of stability. As you root yourself, allow your sensual desires to emerge, embracing them without judgment or shame.

2. Sacral Chakra: Nurturing Creativity
Move up to your sacral chakra, situated in your lower abdomen. Picture a warm, orange light radiating from this energy center, awakening your creative and sensual energies. Explore your fantasies, embracing them as a source of inspiration and empowerment.

3. Solar Plexus Chakra: Confidence and Personal Power
Shift your focus to the solar plexus chakra, located just above your navel. Imagine a glowing yellow light filling this energy center, igniting your confidence and personal power. As you connect with your sensuality, believe in yourself and your desires, allowing them to empower and guide you.

4. Heart Chakra: Unconditional Love and Acceptance
Bring your attention to the heart chakra, situated in the center of your chest.
Visualize a gentle green light emanating from this energy center, representing
love and acceptance. Embrace your sensual desires with compassion and self-
love, knowing that they are an integral part of who you are.

5. Throat Chakra: Expressing Desires
Embrace your voice and let it guide you towards fulfilling your sensual
desires.

Moving to the throat chakra, located in your throat area, imagine a soothing
blue light enveloping this energy center. Allow yourself to speak your desires
and fantasies, expressing them with clarity and authenticity.

Conclusion:
Chakra Bonding Meditations offer sissy babies a transformative path towards
connecting with their sensual desires and fantasies. By engaging with these
powerful energy centers, sissy babies can embrace their true selves, free from
judgment and shame. Through this journey, sissy babies can cultivate self-
love, confidence, and a deeper understanding of their sensuality, ultimately
empowering them to embrace their fantasies and live authentically.

Gratitude Sharing meditations

In this subchapter, we delve into the transformative power of gratitude and
how it can enhance the journey of sissy babies as they connect with their
sensual desires and fantasies. Gratitude sharing meditations offer a unique
approach to explore and embrace the beauty of sensuality within the realm of
sissy baby play.

As sissy babies, it is essential to create a safe and nurturing space where we
can explore our innermost desires without judgment. These meditations guide
us towards a deeper understanding and appreciation of ourselves, our fantasies,
and the world around us. By cultivating gratitude, we open ourselves up to a

wealth of sensual experiences and embrace our fantasies with love and acceptance.

Gratitude sharing meditations begin by acknowledging the gifts and blessings that surround us. Through these practices, we recognize the beauty and pleasure that sensuality brings into our lives. We learn to appreciate the unique qualities that make us who we are, fostering self-love and acceptance.

With each meditation, we explore different aspects of our sensual desires and fantasies, uncovering hidden depths within ourselves. We express gratitude for the feelings, sensations, and experiences that arise during our exploration, allowing ourselves to fully immerse in the joy and pleasure they bring.

Gratitude sharing meditations also encourage us to extend our appreciation beyond ourselves. We acknowledge and express gratitude for the partners, playmates, and communities that support and celebrate our journey. By sharing our gratitude, we strengthen the bonds within our chosen communities, creating a network of love, acceptance, and encouragement.

Through the practice of gratitude, sissy babies can tap into the transformative power of positive energy. As we cultivate gratitude and embrace our fantasies, we become more attuned to our sensuality. We learn to trust our desires and gain the confidence to explore them fully, free from societal constraints and judgment.

Embracing gratitude sharing meditations opens the door to a world of self-discovery and sensual pleasure. By connecting with our desires and fantasies, we create a sacred space where we can freely express ourselves, finding joy and fulfillment in our journey as sissy babies. So, let us embark on this transformative path together, embracing gratitude and celebrating our sensuality with open hearts.

Mirror Movement Meditations

In the realm of self-exploration and personal growth, mirror movement meditations offer a unique and transformative experience for sissy babies to connect with their sensual desires and fantasies. These meditative practices provide a safe space to embrace and explore the depths of your sensuality while fostering self-acceptance and self-love.

Mirror movement meditations invite you to use your reflection as a portal to your inner world. By engaging in gentle and deliberate movements in front of a mirror, you can tap into your sensual essence and unlock hidden desires that may have been suppressed or overlooked. Through this process, you will discover that your fantasies are not only valid but also an essential part of your identity.

These meditations encourage you to embrace the beauty of your body and the power it holds. As a sissy baby, it is crucial to acknowledge and honor your unique sensual nature. Mirror movement meditations allow you to witness your body in motion, appreciating the curves, the softness, and the femininity that define you. By acknowledging and celebrating your physicality, you will cultivate a deeper connection with your sensual self.

During these meditative practices, you will be guided to explore various movements that reflect your fantasies and desires. Whether it is the graceful sway of a dance or the sensuous touch of your own skin, mirror movement meditations encourage you to express your sensuality in a way that feels authentic and empowering to you. By allowing yourself to indulge in these fantasies, you will tap into a wellspring of pleasure and joy that can bring profound fulfillment.

Through regular practice, mirror movement meditations can help sissy babies build a stronger connection between their external and internal worlds. By embracing your fantasies and desires, you will develop a deeper understanding of your own sensuality and its role in your life. This newfound self-awareness will not only enrich your personal relationships but also empower you to navigate the world with confidence and authenticity.

In conclusion, mirror movement meditations offer sissy babies a transformative journey towards self-acceptance, self-love, and sensual exploration. By utilizing the mirror as a tool for self-reflection, these meditative practices allow you to embrace your fantasies and desires, honoring your unique sensual nature. Through deliberate movements and deepening awareness, you will cultivate a profound connection with your sensuality, unlocking a world of pleasure and fulfillment. Embrace your fantasies, dear sissy baby, and let mirror movement meditations guide you on a path of self-discovery and empowerment.

Vulnerability Sharing Meditations

In the enchanting journey of self-discovery and embracing your sensuality, vulnerability is the precious key that unlocks the doors to your deepest desires and fantasies. Welcome to the realm of vulnerability sharing meditations, where sissy babies can connect with their sensual desires in a safe and nurturing space.

For sissy babies, vulnerability is often seen as a weakness or something to be hidden away. However, it is in vulnerability that true strength lies. Through vulnerability sharing meditations, you will learn to embrace your authentic self and open up to the sensual world that awaits you.

These meditations will guide you towards a profound understanding of your desires, allowing you to explore the depths of your fantasies without shame or judgment. By sharing your vulnerabilities with yourself and, if you choose, with trusted partners or a supportive community, you will discover the power of vulnerability as a catalyst for sensual growth.

Through these meditations, you will learn to cultivate self-acceptance, self-love, and self-expression. You will be encouraged to explore the sensual fantasies that have been longing to be acknowledged and experienced. By embracing vulnerability, you will find the courage to step into your desires and create a life that is deeply fulfilling and authentic.

These meditations will provide you with practical tools and techniques to navigate the landscape of vulnerability. You will learn to communicate your desires, set boundaries, and build trust with yourself and others. Through guided visualizations, affirmations, and journaling exercises, you will uncover the layers of conditioning that have kept you from fully embracing your sensuality.

Remember, vulnerability is a gift that allows you to connect with others on a profound level. By sharing your authentic self, you create space for others to do the same. In vulnerability, you will find a community of sissy babies who understand and celebrate your desires, creating a nurturing and empowering environment for growth.

So, dear sissy babies, let us embark on this transformative journey together. Through vulnerability sharing meditations, we will unlock the doors to our sensual desires and fantasies, embracing our true selves with love, acceptance, and unapologetic passion. Get ready to step into a world of sensuality beyond your wildest dreams.

Chapter 4: Embracing Sensuality in Daily Life

Sensual Self-Care Practices

In this subchapter, we will explore the transformative power of sensual self-care practices for sissy babies. By embracing your fantasies and connecting with your sensual desires, you can embark on a journey of self-discovery and personal growth. Through these meditations, you will learn to embrace your true self, indulging in the pleasures that bring you joy and fulfillment.

Sissy babies often find solace and empowerment in their sensual desires and fantasies. These desires are an integral part of who they are, and it is essential to honor and nurture them. Sensual self-care practices provide a safe space to explore and express these desires, allowing sissy babies to connect with their innermost fantasies without judgment or shame.

One powerful practice is creating a sensual sanctuary, a dedicated space where you can fully embrace your fantasies and desires. Decorate this space with soft pillows, scented candles, and beautiful lingerie that makes you feel confident and alluring. Engage in meditation or deep breathing exercises in this sanctuary, allowing yourself to fully embrace and accept your sensual side.

Another practice that can nourish your sensual desires is indulging in sensory experiences. Experiment with different textures, scents, tastes, and sounds that arouse your senses. Take luxurious baths, savor decadent chocolates, or listen to erotic music that resonates with your desires. These experiences can help you tap into the depths of your sensuality, allowing you to fully immerse yourself in your fantasies.

Additionally, self-pleasure rituals can be powerful tools for sissy babies to connect with their sensuality. Engaging in self-exploration and masturbation can provide a gateway to understanding your deepest desires and fantasies.

Through these intimate acts, you can learn to embrace and celebrate your unique sensuality, free from societal expectations or limitations.

Remember, embracing your fantasies and connecting with your sensual desires is a personal journey. It is essential to approach these practices with self-compassion and self-acceptance. Allow yourself the freedom to explore and discover what truly brings you pleasure and fulfillment.

By embracing your fantasies and engaging in sensual self-care practices, you can cultivate a deep sense of self-love and acceptance. These meditations will guide you on a path of self-discovery and empowerment, allowing you to fully embrace your sensual desires as a sissy baby. Embrace your fantasies, for they are essential to your growth and happiness.

Creating a Sensual Self-Care Routine

As sissy babies, it is essential to embrace and nurture our sensual desires and fantasies. One powerful way to do this is by creating a sensual self-care routine that allows us to connect with our deepest sensuality. This subchapter will guide you through various meditations and practices that will help you explore and embrace your sensual self.

The first step in creating a sensual self-care routine is to set aside dedicated time for yourself. Find a quiet and comfortable space where you can be alone and undisturbed. This space should be free from distractions, allowing you to fully immerse yourself in the experience. Consider using soft lighting, scented candles, or calming music to enhance the ambiance.

Begin your sensual self-care routine by focusing on your breath. Close your eyes, take deep breaths, and allow yourself to relax. As you breathe, imagine inhaling positive energy and exhaling any stress or tension. This simple practice will help you ground yourself and create a sense of calm.

Next, explore your body through gentle touch. Start by caressing your skin, paying attention to the sensations it brings. Notice the texture, warmth, and softness of your skin. As you touch yourself, let go of any judgment or self-doubt. Remember, this is a safe space for you to fully embrace your sensual desires.

Incorporate sensual elements into your routine, such as using scented oils or lotions. These can enhance your sensory experience and create an indulgent atmosphere. As you apply these products, focus on the sensations they generate, allowing yourself to fully immerse in the pleasure they provide.

Another powerful practice is visualization. Imagine yourself in your ideal sensual fantasy, exploring your desires without judgment or inhibition. Picture yourself embracing your fantasies, feeling confident, beautiful, and desired. Visualization allows you to connect with your deepest sensual desires and helps bring them to life.

Finally, conclude your sensual self-care routine with a moment of reflection and gratitude. Take a few moments to appreciate yourself and the journey you are on. Embrace your sensuality and your ability to connect with your desires. Express gratitude for the opportunity to explore and nurture your sensual self.

Creating a sensual self-care routine as a sissy baby is an empowering and transformative practice. By dedicating time to connect with your sensual desires and fantasies, you embrace your authentic self and nurture your sensuality. Embrace this journey, and let it guide you towards a deeper connection with your true desires and a greater sense of self-acceptance.

Exploring Sensual Bathing Rituals

Welcome to the subchapter on "Exploring Sensual Bathing Rituals" from the book "Embracing Your Fantasies: Meditations for Sissy Babies on Sensuality." This chapter is exclusively designed for sissy babies who yearn to connect with their sensual desires and fantasies through the art of bathing.

Bathing is not merely a routine task but a sacred ritual that allows you to immerse yourself in sensuality, self-care, and self-discovery. It offers you a sanctuary, a safe space where you can explore and embrace your deepest desires without judgment or inhibition.

To embark on this transformative journey, create an ambiance that stimulates your senses. Dim the lights, light aromatic candles, and play soft, soothing music. Fill your bathtub with warm water infused with aromatic oils or bath salts that resonate with your fantasies. Allow the fragrances to transport you to a world of sensuality and pleasure.

As you step into the water, surrender yourself to the moment. Close your eyes and let your mind wander to places that excite you. Visualize your desires, your fantasies, and imagine yourself embodying them completely. Feel the water caress your skin, cleansing away any inhibitions or shame.

Explore different textures and sensations during your bath. Use luxurious sponges, soft brushes, or even silk scarves to gently stroke your body. Let your hands wander, embracing every curve and contour, and revel in the pleasure that arises from self-touch and self-exploration.

Engage all your senses during this ritual. Savor the taste of decadent chocolates or fruits, allowing the flavors to complement the sensations of the bath. Listen to the sound of water, the music, or your own breath, letting them guide you deeper into your sensuality.

As the water drains away, let go of any guilt or shame associated with your desires. Embrace them as an integral part of your being, an expression of your authentic self. Use this sacred time to reaffirm your sensual identity and to connect with your true desires.

Remember, sissy baby, that sensuality is not something to be ashamed of. By embracing your fantasies and connecting with your sensual desires, you are empowering yourself and embracing your own unique journey of self-discovery and self-love. So, indulge in these bathing rituals, and let them guide you towards a deeper understanding and acceptance of your sensual nature.

Nurturing the Sissy Baby Within

Welcome, dear sissy babies, to the subchapter titled "Nurturing the Sissy Baby Within" in our book, "Embracing Your Fantasies: Meditations for Sissy Babies on Sensuality." In this section, we will explore how you can connect with your sensual desires and fantasies, allowing the sissy baby within you to flourish and thrive.

As sissy babies, you have a unique and beautiful way of experiencing sensuality. It is a journey of self-discovery and self-acceptance, where you can fully embrace your desires without judgment or shame. By nurturing the sissy baby within, you create a safe and loving space to explore your deepest fantasies.

Meditation plays a significant role in this process. Through meditation, you can connect with your inner self, allowing your desires to unfold naturally. Find a quiet and comfortable place where you can relax and let your mind wander. Close your eyes, take deep breaths, and visualize your sissy baby self surrounded by a warm and loving light. Allow yourself to feel safe and supported in this space.

During these meditations, focus on understanding your desires and fantasies. What excites you? What makes you feel sensual and alive? Allow these thoughts to flow freely, without judgment or inhibition. Embrace them fully, knowing that they are an essential part of who you are.

Nurturing the sissy baby within also involves self-care and self-expression. Explore different ways to pamper yourself, whether it be through indulging in luxurious bubble baths, dressing up in your favorite sissy baby attire, or engaging in sensual activities that bring you pleasure. Embrace your femininity and allow it to manifest in every aspect of your life.

Furthermore, find a community of like-minded individuals who share similar desires and fantasies. Connect with other sissy babies who can offer support, understanding, and guidance on this journey. Online forums, chat groups, or local meetups can provide a safe space for you to express yourself and learn from others' experiences.

Remember, dear sissy babies, that embracing your fantasies and connecting with your sensual desires is a beautiful and empowering process. By nurturing the sissy baby within, you can tap into a profound sense of self-acceptance, love, and joy. Embrace your inner sissy baby, and let your fantasies guide you towards a life of sensuality and fulfillment.

Sensual Dressing and Fashion

In this subchapter, we will explore the transformative power of dressing sensually and how it can help sissy babies connect with their deepest desires and fantasies. Fashion has long been recognized as a means of self-expression, and for sissy babies, it can serve as a gateway to explore their sensuality in a safe and empowering way.

Sissy babies often find solace in embracing their femininity and expressing their sensual desires through clothing choices. By carefully selecting fabrics, colors, and styles that resonate with their personal fantasies, sissy babies can create a world where their sensuality can flourish. Whether it's the feel of satin against their skin, the swish of a flowing skirt, or the delicate touch of lace, each garment becomes a tool for self-discovery and pleasure.

Meditation plays a crucial role in this journey, as it allows sissy babies to connect with their inner desires and explore their fantasies in a contemplative and introspective manner. By combining meditation with fashion, sissy babies can enter a state of mindfulness where they can fully embrace their sensual selves and find joy in their unique desires.

It is essential for sissy babies to create a safe and non-judgmental space for themselves when exploring sensual dressing and fashion. This may involve setting aside dedicated time for self-reflection, creating a private dressing area, or seeking support from like-minded individuals who can offer guidance and encouragement. By cultivating an environment that fosters self-acceptance and self-love, sissy babies can confidently embrace their fantasies and sensuality.

Furthermore, the act of dressing sensually can be seen as a form of self-care. It allows sissy babies to prioritize their own pleasure and well-being. Feeling beautiful and desirable in their chosen outfits can boost self-confidence and enhance their overall sense of self-worth.

In conclusion, sensual dressing and fashion offer sissy babies a unique pathway to connect with their inner desires and fantasies. By combining meditation, self-reflection, and a non-judgmental approach, sissy babies can explore their sensuality in a safe and empowering manner. Through the careful selection of garments that resonate with their fantasies, sissy babies can create a world where their sensual desires can thrive, ultimately leading to self-acceptance, self-love, and a deeper connection with their true selves.

Expressing Sensuality through Clothing Choices

In the world of sensuality and self-expression, clothing choices play a vital role. For sissy babies, exploring their sensual desires and fantasies can be a transformative journey. The way we dress has the power to enhance our confidence, embrace our fantasies, and connect with our sensual selves on a deeper level.

Clothing serves as a gateway to exploring our inner desires and expressing them outwardly. It becomes a means of communication between our sensual desires and the outside world. By carefully choosing the right garments, sissy babies can create a visual representation of their sensuality, allowing them to fully embrace their fantasies.

When it comes to expressing sensuality through clothing, there are no set rules or limitations. It is a personal journey that is unique to each individual. Some sissy babies may find joy in adorning themselves with delicate lace, frills, and bows, while others may prefer the feeling of satin and silk against their skin. The key is to embrace what feels right and comfortable for you.

Exploring different styles and fabrics can be a meditative experience for sissy babies. It allows them to connect with their sensual desires and fantasies in a safe and nurturing way. Each garment can be seen as an invitation to explore different aspects of their sensuality, whether it be the feeling of a soft fabric against their body or the visual representation of their desires.

It is important to remember that clothing choices are not limited to the bedroom. Sissy babies can express their sensuality and fantasies in their everyday lives as well. Whether it is a subtle hint of lace peeking out from under a shirt or a daring outfit that embraces their desires, the choice is theirs to make.

By embracing their fantasies and connecting with their sensual desires through clothing, sissy babies can experience a sense of liberation and empowerment. It allows them to embrace their authentic selves and break free from societal constraints. Through their clothing choices, they can create a world where sensuality and fantasy intertwine, giving birth to a new and exciting self-expression.

In conclusion, expressing sensuality through clothing choices is a powerful tool for sissy babies to connect with their sensual desires and fantasies. It is a journey of self-discovery and empowerment, where each garment becomes a sacred invitation to explore their innermost desires. By embracing their fantasies and expressing themselves through clothing, sissy babies can create a world where their sensual desires are celebrated and cherished.

Exploring Different Styles and Fabrics

In the enchanting world of sensuality and self-expression, sissy babies have the opportunity to delve into a realm of endless possibilities. This subchapter, "Exploring Different Styles and Fabrics," invites you, dear sissy baby, to embark on a journey of discovery, unveiling the captivating variety of styles and fabrics that can enhance your sensual desires and fantasies.

Styles, oh how they can transform us! From delicate and feminine to bold and daring, every sissy baby has their unique taste and preferences. Take time to explore different styles that resonate with your essence, allowing them to become an extension of your sensuality. Whether it's the elegance of a frilly, lace-trimmed dress or the playfulness of a ruffled romper, each style has its own enchanting allure. Embrace the freedom to experiment with different looks, allowing your inner desires to guide you towards the styles that make you feel most connected to your sensual self.

Fabrics hold a special place in the realm of sensuality. They have the ability to evoke emotions, tantalize the senses, and bring fantasies to life. Silky satin, with its smooth and luxurious touch, can awaken your desires and ignite a fire within you. Delve into the world of lace, a fabric that whispers secrets and adds a touch of sensuality to any garment it adorns. The sensuous embrace of velvet against your skin invites you to embrace your desires with a newfound confidence. The choices are endless, and each fabric holds the potential to unlock a different aspect of your sensuality.

As you explore different styles and fabrics, remember that this journey is about embracing your fantasies and connecting with your sensuality. Allow yourself the freedom to let go of any inhibitions or judgments. This is your sacred space, where you can fully express who you are and what brings you pleasure.

Experiment, play, and revel in the joy of discovering the styles and fabrics that resonate with your sensual desires. Embrace the power they hold to awaken your senses and transport you to a world where your fantasies come to life.

Remember, dear sissy baby, your sensuality is a gift to be cherished and celebrated. Embrace it with open arms and let it guide you on a path of self-discovery and fulfillment.

So, go forth, dear sissy baby, and immerse yourself in the enchanting world of different styles and fabrics. Allow them to become the canvas upon which you paint your sensual desires and fantasies, embracing every moment of the journey with a sense of wonder and delight.

Building a Sensual Wardrobe

In the journey towards embracing your sensuality, one aspect that cannot be overlooked is the importance of a carefully curated wardrobe. Your clothing choices can be a powerful tool in connecting with your desires and fantasies as a sissy baby. This subchapter will guide you on how to build a sensual wardrobe that truly reflects your innermost sensual desires.

When it comes to building your sensual wardrobe, it is essential to prioritize comfort and self-expression. Begin by selecting fabrics that feel soft and luxurious against your skin. Embrace satin, lace, and silk materials that exude sensuality and elegance. These fabrics will not only enhance your physical sensations but also awaken your senses, allowing you to fully immerse yourself in the world of your fantasies.

Colors also play a significant role in setting the mood. Explore a range of colors that resonate with your desires, whether it be delicate pastels, bold reds, or seductive blacks. Each color has its own unique energy, and by consciously choosing the shades that evoke your desires, you can create a wardrobe that truly reflects your sensual self.

Incorporating lingerie into your wardrobe is a vital step towards embracing your sensuality. Delicate bras, panties, and garter belts can make you feel feminine and empowered. Experiment with different styles, from classic to more daring pieces, and find what makes you feel most confident and alluring.

Remember, your sensual wardrobe is a personal expression of your desires, so don't be afraid to explore and try new things.

Accessories are the finishing touch that completes any outfit and enhances your sensual persona. Add a touch of glamour with delicate jewelry, such as necklaces, bracelets, or earrings. Experiment with stockings, heels, and gloves to further enhance the sensual experience. These small details can greatly contribute to your overall transformation and help you connect with your fantasies on a deeper level.

As you build your sensual wardrobe, it is important to remember that this is a journey of self-discovery and self-acceptance. Embrace your desires, explore your fantasies, and allow your wardrobe to be a reflection of your most authentic self. By connecting with your sensuality through your clothing choices, you are taking a powerful step towards embracing your fantasies and finding true fulfillment as a sissy baby.

Chapter 5: Embracing Sensuality in Relationships

Communicating Sensual Desires with Partners

In the enchanting world of sensuality, exploring and embracing your desires can be an exhilarating journey. As sissy babies, understanding and communicating your sensual needs with your partners can lead to powerful connections and a deeper understanding of your fantasies. This subchapter aims to guide you through the art of expressing your desires, fostering trust, and creating a safe space for exploration.

Effective communication is the key to unlocking the magical realm of sensuality. It allows you to share your deepest longings, bringing you closer to your partner and enabling them to understand your desires. Begin by cultivating self-awareness. Take time to explore your innermost desires, fantasies, and fetishes. Reflect on what truly arouses you and what you yearn for in an intimate encounter.

Once you have gained clarity, it's essential to find the right words to express yourself. Start by setting the stage for open and honest communication. Create a safe and non-judgmental space where both you and your partner can freely express your desires. Trust is crucial here, as vulnerability is an inherent part of sharing your sensual needs.

When the time feels right, gently introduce your desires to your partner. Begin with a calm and loving conversation, expressing your appreciation for their presence in your life. Use "I" statements to convey your feelings and desires, ensuring that your words are focused on your own experiences rather than making assumptions or placing blame.

Remember that your partner may have their own desires and boundaries. Be open to their responses and willing to listen to their needs as well. This is a two-way street, and mutual understanding is essential for a healthy and fulfilling relationship.

As you embark on this journey of communication, keep in mind that it may take time for your partner to fully comprehend and embrace your desires. Patience, compassion, and open-mindedness will go a long way in nurturing the connection between you.

In conclusion, communicating your sensual desires with your partner is an empowering and transformative experience. By cultivating self-awareness, creating a safe space, and fostering trust, you can embark on a journey of shared exploration and fulfillment. Embrace the beauty of your fantasies, and allow them to guide you towards deeper connections and a more profound understanding of your sensuality.

Building Trust and Openness

In the journey of embracing your fantasies and connecting with your sensual desires, building trust and openness is a crucial step for sissy babies. Trusting yourself and others, as well as fostering an environment of openness, can unlock the true potential of your sensual exploration. This subchapter explores key elements that contribute to building trust and openness, allowing you to fully embrace your fantasies.

Trusting yourself is the foundation of any personal growth. As a sissy baby, it is essential to trust your instincts and desires. Acknowledge and embrace your fantasies without judgment or shame. Understand that your sensual desires are unique and valid. By trusting yourself, you can begin to explore your fantasies with confidence and authenticity.

Building trust with others is equally important. Identifying individuals who are supportive and understanding of your journey is crucial. Seek out trustworthy friends, partners, or communities that provide a safe space for you to express yourself openly. Trust is built over time, so take your time to find those who genuinely respect and appreciate your unique desires.

Openness is the key to unlocking the full potential of your sensual exploration. To foster openness, practice effective communication. Clearly express your needs, boundaries, and desires to those you trust. By openly sharing your fantasies, you invite others to understand and respect your sensual journey.

It is important to remember that building trust and openness is a continuous process. Be patient with yourself and others as you navigate this path of self-discovery. Celebrate each step forward, no matter how small, and learn from any setbacks. Remember, your sensual desires are a beautiful part of who you are, deserving of love and acceptance.

In conclusion, building trust and openness is essential for sissy babies to fully embrace their sensual desires and fantasies. Trusting yourself and others, and fostering an environment of openness, allows for authentic exploration. By acknowledging and embracing your unique desires, and finding trustworthy individuals and communities, you can create a safe space to express yourself openly. Remember, this journey is yours to embrace, and building trust and openness will help you unlock the true potential of your sensual exploration.

Initiating Conversations about Sensuality

As sissy babies, it is crucial to embrace and explore our sensuality in a safe and supportive environment. This subchapter aims to guide you through the process of initiating conversations about sensuality, enabling you to connect with your deepest desires and fantasies. By engaging in meditations specifically designed for sissy babies, we can cultivate a sense of self-acceptance and freedom to explore our sensual nature.

One of the most important steps in this journey is finding a trusted confidante, someone who can understand and support our exploration of sensuality. This person can be a partner, a close friend, or even a therapist who specializes in alternative lifestyles. Opening up to them about our fantasies and desires can be a vulnerable experience, but it is a crucial step towards embracing our true selves.

To initiate these conversations, it is helpful to start by expressing our curiosity and longing for a deeper connection with our sensuality. We may share our desire to explore new experiences or discuss specific fantasies that have been on our minds. By articulating our feelings and desires, we create an opportunity for our confidante to understand us better and provide the support we need.

During these conversations, it is important to remember that sensuality is a personal journey, and everyone's desires are unique. It is essential to communicate our boundaries and establish a safe space where we can explore our fantasies without judgment or shame. By setting clear expectations and discussing consent, we can ensure that all parties involved feel comfortable and respected.

In addition to external conversations, this subchapter also encourages sissy babies to engage in introspective meditations. These meditations can help us connect with our sensual desires on a deep emotional and spiritual level. By focusing on our breath, visualizations, and affirmations, we can tap into our subconscious and unlock hidden desires that we may not have been aware of.

Remember, embracing our fantasies and desires is a courageous act that requires self-acceptance and vulnerability. By initiating conversations about sensuality, both externally and internally, we can embark on a transformative journey of self-discovery and fulfillment. So, let us open up, connect with our sensual desires, and embrace the sissy baby within us, knowing that we are not alone on this beautiful journey.

Negotiating Boundaries and Consent

In the enchanting journey of embracing your sensuality and exploring your deepest desires and fantasies, it is essential to understand the importance of negotiating boundaries and seeking consent. As sissy babies, it is crucial to create a safe and respectful space for ourselves and our partners.

Boundaries are the invisible lines that define our comfort zones, both emotionally and physically. They serve as a guide to ensure that we engage in experiences that align with our desires and limitations. It is essential to communicate these boundaries openly and honestly with our partners, allowing for a deeper understanding and connection.

Negotiating boundaries begins with self-awareness. Take the time to reflect on your desires, fantasies, and limits. What are the activities that excite you? What are the ones that make you uncomfortable? By understanding your own boundaries, you can effectively communicate them to your partner, fostering an environment of trust and respect.

Consent is the cornerstone of any healthy and fulfilling sensual exploration. It is an ongoing process that requires continuous communication and respect for each other's desires and limits. Consent must be enthusiastic, explicit, and freely given by all parties involved. It is crucial to remember that consent can be withdrawn at any time, and it should always be respected without question.

When negotiating boundaries and seeking consent, it is essential to approach the conversation with vulnerability and empathy. Create a safe space where both you and your partner can openly express your desires, fears, and uncertainties. Encourage a non-judgmental atmosphere where each person's boundaries are valued and respected. Remember, negotiation is not about compromising your desires but finding a common ground where both parties feel comfortable and fulfilled.

In the realm of sensual exploration, it is also fundamental to understand that boundaries and consent extend beyond the physical realm. Emotional boundaries are just as crucial in creating a safe and nurturing space. It is essential to communicate your emotional needs and boundaries, ensuring that your partner understands and respects them.

By embracing negotiation and consent, sissy babies can embark on a journey of sensual exploration that is fulfilling, empowering, and respectful. The journey towards self-discovery and pleasure is one that should be embarked upon with care, love, and mutual understanding. So, dear sissy babies, let us honor our desires, respect our boundaries, and embrace the beauty of negotiating consent as we delve into the enchanting world of our sensuality and fantasies.

Exploring Sensuality with a Partner

In the journey of embracing your fantasies and connecting with your sensual desires, exploring sensuality with a partner can be a transformative experience for sissy babies. By opening up to a trusted partner, you can deepen your understanding of your own desires, enhance your connection, and create a space where your fantasies can flourish.

The exploration of sensuality with a partner begins with open and honest communication. Trust and consent are paramount. It is important to find a partner who is understanding, non-judgmental, and willing to explore with you. Communicate your desires, boundaries, and fantasies, ensuring that both parties are comfortable and enthusiastic about the experience.

Once you have established a foundation of trust, embark on a journey of self-discovery together. Experiment with different sensory experiences that arouse your senses. Explore the power of touch, taste, sound, sight, and smell to heighten your sensations. Allow your partner to explore your body and discover what brings you pleasure. Together, you can navigate the nuances of your desires and find new ways to indulge in sensuality.

Create a safe and inviting space for your exploration. Set the mood with soft lighting, scented candles, and soothing music. Engage in activities that awaken your senses, such as sensual massages, role-playing, or dress-up. Allow yourself to fully immerse in the experience and let your fantasies come to life.

Remember, sensuality is not solely focused on sexual acts but encompasses a broader spectrum of intimate connection. Embrace the power of emotional intimacy and vulnerability with your partner. Share your deepest desires and fantasies, and encourage them to do the same. By nurturing a strong emotional bond, you can enhance your sensual experiences and create a space where fantasies can be explored without judgment.

As you embark on this journey together, be open to new experiences and willing to push boundaries, always with the understanding and consent of both partners. Embrace the beauty of connecting with your sensual desires and fantasies, allowing them to guide you towards self-discovery and personal growth.

In conclusion, exploring sensuality with a partner is a profound and empowering experience for sissy babies. By nurturing trust, communication, and consent, you can create a safe and inviting space to indulge in your fantasies. Embrace the power of sensual touch, emotional intimacy, and sensory experiences to deepen your connection and explore new realms of pleasure. Remember, this journey is about self-discovery, growth, and embracing the beauty of your desires.

Sensual Role-Playing and Fantasies

Sensual Role-Playing and Fantasies: Exploring Your Inner Desires

Welcome to the subchapter on "Sensual Role-Playing and Fantasies" from the book "Embracing Your Fantasies: Meditations for Sissy Babies on Sensuality." This chapter is dedicated to sissy babies who are looking to connect with their sensual desires and explore the realm of role-playing and fantasies.

Role-playing and indulging in fantasies can be a powerful tool for self-exploration and self-expression. It allows sissy babies to step outside their daily routines and embrace a different persona, unlocking hidden desires and passions. This journey of self-discovery can be both thrilling and liberating.

Within the realm of sensual role-playing, one can become anyone they desire. Whether it's a submissive maid, a seductive mistress, or an innocent princess, the possibilities are endless. Engaging in these scenarios allows sissy babies to tap into their sensual side and experience pleasure in a safe and consensual manner.

To begin your exploration, it's important to establish trust and open communication with your partner. Discuss your desires, boundaries, and consent before delving into any role-playing scenario. Remember, this is a journey of self-discovery and pleasure, so both you and your partner should feel comfortable and respected throughout the experience.

Start by identifying your fantasies. What scenarios or characters excite you? Is it the idea of being dominated, nurturing, or perhaps a combination of both? Take the time to understand your desires and embrace them without judgment. Remember, fantasies are a normal part of human sexuality.

Once you've identified your fantasies, create a safe and inviting space to explore them. Set the mood with sensual lighting, music, or props that align with your desired scenario. As you immerse yourself in the role, allow yourself to fully embrace the character and let go of inhibitions. This is your chance to live out your fantasies and experience pleasure in a way that feels authentic to you.

Throughout this journey, remember that sensual role-playing and fantasies are about self-discovery and pleasure. Embrace your desires, explore new horizons, and let your imagination run wild. By connecting with your sensual side, you'll find a deeper understanding of your authentic self and experience the joy and fulfillment that comes with embracing your fantasies.

So, dear sissy babies, take this opportunity to dive into the world of sensual role-playing and fantasies. Unleash your desires, explore new realms, and embrace the pleasure that awaits you. This is your chance to connect with your deepest sensual desires and discover the authentic, sensual being within you. Enjoy the journey, and may it bring you endless joy and satisfaction.

Introducing Sensual Toys and Accessories

In this subchapter, we delve into the exciting world of sensual toys and accessories, designed to enhance your experience as a sissy baby exploring your sensual desires and fantasies. These delightful additions can help you connect with your innermost sensual self, allowing you to fully embrace and indulge in your fantasies.

Sensual toys and accessories serve as powerful tools to unlock new dimensions of pleasure, whether you choose to enjoy them alone or with a partner. They come in various shapes, sizes, and functionalities, catering to a wide range of preferences and desires. These items are carefully crafted to provide stimulation to erogenous zones, intensify pleasure, and stimulate your senses, ultimately opening doors to unimaginable sensations.

One of the most popular sensual toys is the vibrator. With its ability to provide intense vibrations to various parts of your body, it can be an excellent addition to your sensual journey. From clitoral stimulators to anal vibrators, there is a wide array of options to explore, each offering a unique sensation that can transport you to new heights of pleasure.

For those interested in experimenting with different types of sensations, sensory play toys such as feather ticklers, blindfolds, and restraints can be incredibly enticing. These accessories heighten your senses, allowing you to focus solely on the pleasure coursing through your body. By relinquishing control and surrendering to the sensations, you can fully immerse yourself in your sissy baby persona and embrace the sensuality within.

Additionally, there are specialized toys designed to cater specifically to sissy babies, such as pacifiers and adult-sized baby bottles. These items can help you tap into your inner child and explore the nurturing and comforting aspects of your fantasies. They provide a sense of security, allowing you to fully let go and connect with your sensual desires, free from any inhibitions or judgment.

Remember, the key to a fulfilling sensual journey lies in exploring your desires and boundaries at your own pace. Take the time to educate yourself about these toys and accessories, ensuring they are safe, comfortable, and suitable for your needs. Communication with your partner, if applicable, is also crucial to ensure a shared understanding and consent when incorporating these items into your sensual play.

Embrace the world of sensual toys and accessories, sissy babies, and allow them to guide you on a journey of self-discovery, pleasure, and fulfillment. By embracing your fantasies and desires, you can unleash the sensual being within, experiencing a newfound sense of liberation and connection to your sensuality.

Enhancing Intimacy through Sensual Techniques

Intimacy is a vital aspect of any relationship, allowing partners to establish a deep connection and explore their desires and fantasies together. For sissy babies, embracing their sensual desires and fantasies is an essential part of their journey towards self-discovery and self-acceptance. In this subchapter, we will delve into various sensual techniques that can help sissy babies enhance their intimacy and connect with their deepest desires.

1. Sensual Touch: Touch is a powerful tool for building intimacy and exploring sensuality. Experiment with different textures, such as silk or feathers, to awaken your senses. Engage in sensual massages with your partner, focusing on areas that bring you pleasure. Don't forget to communicate your preferences and boundaries, ensuring a safe and comfortable experience for both you and your partner.

2. Role-Playing: Role-playing allows sissy babies to step into different personas and explore their fantasies. Embrace your inner desires and communicate with your partner about your fantasies. Whether it's playing the obedient sissy or the dominant mistress, engaging in role-playing can strengthen the bond with your partner and enable you to fully embrace your sensuality.

3. Sensory Play: Sensory play involves indulging in different sensations to heighten pleasure. Experiment with blindfolds, scented candles, or soothing music to create an intimate atmosphere. Explore the power of anticipation and surprise, letting your senses guide you towards a heightened state of sensual pleasure.

4. Communication and Consent: Open and honest communication is the key to fostering intimacy. Discuss your desires, boundaries, and fantasies with your partner, ensuring that you both feel comfortable and respected. Prioritize consent in every aspect of your sensual exploration, creating a safe space where you can freely express yourself without judgment.

5. Self-Exploration: Before you can fully embrace your sensuality with a partner, it's important to explore and understand your own desires. Take time for self-reflection and meditation, allowing yourself to delve into your fantasies and discover what truly brings you pleasure. Embrace your inner sissy baby and embrace the beauty of your desires.

Remember, enhancing intimacy through sensual techniques is a personal journey that requires self-acceptance, open communication, and respect.

Embrace your fantasies, connect with your sensual desires, and allow yourself to fully indulge in the world of sensuality. By doing so, you can strengthen your relationships, experience deeper connections, and ultimately embrace your truest self as a sissy baby.

Chapter 6: Embracing Sensuality Beyond the Bedroom

Sensuality in Everyday Activities

In the journey of embracing your fantasies, it is essential to explore sensuality in everyday activities. As sissy babies, it is crucial to connect with your inner desires and fantasies, allowing yourself to fully experience the richness of sensuality in every facet of your life. By immersing yourself in this exploration, you can cultivate a deeper connection with your sensual self and enhance your overall well-being.

Meditations for sissy babies to connect with their sensual desires and fantasies offer a gateway to unlock the hidden realms of pleasure and self-discovery. Through these meditations, you will learn to embrace sensuality in the most ordinary activities, transforming them into extraordinary experiences that nourish your mind, body, and soul.

Let us delve into some everyday activities that can be transformed into sensual rituals:

1. Bathing Rituals: Transform your daily bath into a sacred experience by incorporating scented candles, aromatic oils, and soft music. Focus on the sensation of water caressing your skin, allowing your body to relax and release any tension. Feel the warmth of the water enveloping you, awakening your senses and connecting you with your sensuality.

2. Cooking as an Art: Turn cooking into a sensual adventure by indulging in the textures, scents, and tastes of ingredients. Allow your senses to guide you as you chop, sauté, and stir. Experiment with flavors, savoring each bite mindfully. Cooking becomes a dance of pleasure, where you connect with your sensual desires through the creation of delectable dishes.

3. Mindful Movement: Engage in activities like yoga, dance, or even a simple walk in nature. As you move your body, pay attention to the sensations, the rhythm, and the flow. Let the movement become a form of self-expression, a sensual exploration of your physicality, and a celebration of your sensuality.

4. Sensual Self-Care: Embrace self-care rituals that nourish your body and delight your senses. Pamper yourself with luxurious body oils, perfumes, and silky fabrics. Engage in activities like self-massage, indulgent baths, or even dressing in sensual attire that makes you feel beautiful and desirable. These acts of self-love and care are pathways to connect with your sensuality.

By incorporating sensuality into your everyday activities, you will discover a deeper connection with your desires and fantasies as a sissy baby. These meditations will guide you on a transformative journey, allowing you to fully embrace your sensuality and unlock the true fulfillment that lies within. So, dear sissy babies, immerse yourselves in the richness of sensuality and let it guide you towards a life of pleasure and self-discovery.

Cultivating Mindful Eating

In the fast-paced world we live in, it's easy to get caught up in the chaos and neglect the simple act of eating. However, for sissy babies seeking to connect with their sensual desires and fantasies, mindful eating can be a powerful tool to enhance their experiences. By being fully present and aware during meals, sissy babies can deepen their connection with their sensual selves and explore their fantasies in a new and exciting way.

Mindful eating is about more than just devouring a meal. It is a practice that encourages sissy babies to slow down, savor each bite, and truly appreciate the flavors and textures of the food they consume. By engaging all their senses, sissy babies can tap into a heightened state of awareness and sensuality.

To cultivate mindful eating, sissy babies can start by creating a sacred space for their meals. This could involve setting a beautifully decorated table, playing soft music, or lighting scented candles to create an atmosphere of sensuality and relaxation. By intentionally creating an environment that caters to their desires, sissy babies can fully immerse themselves in the experience.

Before diving into a meal, sissy babies can take a moment to express gratitude for the nourishment they are about to receive. This act of gratitude not only enhances the sensory experience but also helps sissy babies to appreciate the connection between sensuality and self-care.

During the meal, sissy babies can focus on each bite, savoring the flavors and textures as they explore their sensual desires. They can pay attention to how the food feels in their mouth, the aroma that fills the air, and the way it nourishes their body. By engaging all their senses, sissy babies can heighten their sensual experiences and awaken their fantasies.

In addition to being present during meals, sissy babies can also incorporate mindful eating into their daily lives by being conscious of their food choices. By selecting foods that are not only nourishing but also indulgent and pleasurable, sissy babies can further connect with their sensual desires and fantasies.

Cultivating mindful eating is a powerful practice for sissy babies to connect with their sensual selves. By being fully present and aware during meals, sissy babies can explore their desires and fantasies in a way that is both indulgent and nourishing. So, embrace the practice of mindful eating and allow it to guide you on a journey of sensuality and self-discovery.

Engaging the Senses in Nature

Engaging the Senses in Nature: A Sensual Journey for Sissy Babies

In the hustle and bustle of our modern lives, we often forget the importance of connecting with our senses and embracing the beauty of nature. For sissy babies, who yearn for a deeper understanding of their sensual desires and fantasies, engaging the senses in nature can be a transformative experience. It allows them to tap into their innermost desires and explore the depths of their sensuality.

Nature has a unique way of awakening our senses, inviting us to indulge in its seductive allure. The subchapter "Engaging the Senses in Nature" explores various meditations and practices designed to help sissy babies connect with their sensual selves. By immersing themselves in the wonders of the natural world, they can unlock a realm of sensory pleasure and unleash their fantasies.

One powerful meditation involves finding a serene spot in nature, where sissy babies can be alone and undisturbed. They are encouraged to close their eyes and take slow, deep breaths, allowing the fragrant scents of blossoming flowers and fresh earth to fill their lungs. As they breathe in, they visualize their sensual desires, embracing them fully and without judgment.

Another practice involves sissy babies taking barefoot walks on the soft, grassy ground. They are encouraged to pay attention to the sensation of the earth beneath their feet, grounding themselves and connecting with the primal energy of nature. With each step, they can let go of societal expectations and embrace their true selves.

Engaging the senses in nature also involves indulging in the visual feast that surrounds us. Sissy babies are encouraged to observe the vibrant colors of blooming flowers, the dance of sunlight through the leaves, and the gentle sway of grass in the wind. These visual experiences can awaken their sensual desires and transport them to a world where fantasies come alive.

Ultimately, "Engaging the Senses in Nature" is a subchapter that invites sissy babies to explore their sensual desires and fantasies in the embrace of nature. By connecting with their senses and immersing themselves in the beauty that surrounds them, they can tap into a wellspring of sensuality and experience a deeper connection with their true selves. Through meditations and practices tailored for sissy babies, this subchapter provides a roadmap to unlocking their sensual desires and embracing their fantasies in the most natural and fulfilling way possible.

Sensual Creativity and Expression

In this subchapter, we will explore the enchanting realm of sensual creativity and expression, specifically tailored for our beloved sissy babies. As you embark on this journey, remember that embracing your fantasies and desires is a beautiful and empowering experience that can lead to a deeper connection with your authentic self.

Creativity knows no boundaries, and your sensual desires are no exception. By tapping into your inner artist, you can unlock a world of endless possibilities and explore the depths of your sensuality. Through meditations and exercises, we will guide you towards embracing and expressing your unique fantasies in a safe and nurturing environment.

Meditation is a powerful tool for self-discovery and connecting with your desires. By quieting your mind and focusing on your breath, you can access the hidden recesses of your imagination. These meditative practices will allow you to tap into your sensual energy, awakening your deepest desires and fostering self-acceptance.

Through guided visualizations, you will be encouraged to explore different scenarios and sensations, allowing your creativity to flow freely. Whether it's envisioning yourself in delicate lingerie or indulging in luxurious pampering, these visualizations will help you create a vivid and immersive experience that connects you with your sensuality on a profound level.

Expressing your sensuality can take many forms. From writing sensual stories and poetry to creating artwork or experimenting with fashion, there are countless ways to give life to your fantasies. We will provide you with practical exercises and prompts designed to ignite your creative spark and encourage self-expression in a way that feels authentic to you.

Remember, sissy babies, that embracing your fantasies is an act of self-love and self-acceptance. By exploring your sensuality and expressing yourself creatively, you are honoring your desires and cultivating a deeper connection with your truest self. Allow yourself the freedom to explore without judgment or shame, and let your sensual creativity guide you towards a more fulfilling and authentic life.

In the pages that follow, you will find a wealth of inspiration, guidance, and practical exercises to support you on this journey of self-discovery. Embrace your fantasies, dear sissy babies, and let the power of sensual creativity and expression lead you towards a life of joy, pleasure, and unapologetic self-love.

Embracing Sensuality in Public

In our journey towards self-discovery and self-acceptance, it is essential to explore and embrace our sensuality. Sensuality is a natural aspect of human existence, and it should not be confined to the privacy of our bedrooms. This subchapter aims to guide sissy babies on how to connect with their sensual desires and fantasies in public settings.

Society often imposes restrictions and shame around expressing our sensuality, particularly for those who identify as sissy babies. However, it is crucial to remember that embracing our fantasies and desires is an integral part of our personal growth and happiness. By embracing our sensuality, we can unlock a world of pleasure, self-confidence, and freedom.

One way to begin embracing sensuality in public is through meditation. Meditations for sissy babies can be a powerful tool to help connect with your sensual desires and fantasies. Through meditation, you can create a safe and sacred space within yourself, allowing you to explore your sensuality without fear or judgment. Take a few moments each day to sit in a quiet place, focus on your breath, and visualize yourself fully embracing your sensual self in public settings. Allow yourself to feel the power and liberation that comes with expressing your desires openly.

Another technique to embrace sensuality in public is by experimenting with your style and clothing choices. Sissy babies often have a unique sense of fashion, and by expressing yourself through your clothing, you can embody your sensuality. Whether it's incorporating lace, frills, or bold colors into your outfits, embrace your true self without fear of judgment. Remember, confidence is key when it comes to embracing your sensuality in public.

Furthermore, connecting with like-minded individuals can be beneficial for sissy babies seeking to embrace their sensuality. Seek out communities, support groups, or online forums where you can share your experiences and learn from others. Surrounding yourself with people who understand and accept your desires can provide a sense of belonging and empowerment.

Embracing your sensuality in public may be challenging at first, but it is a powerful step towards self-acceptance and living authentically. Through meditations, fashion choices, and connecting with a supportive community, sissy babies can explore their sensual desires and fantasies openly and confidently. Remember, your sensuality is a beautiful part of who you are, and it deserves to be celebrated and embraced in every aspect of your life.

Overcoming Self-Consciousness

In this subchapter, we will explore the powerful journey of overcoming self-consciousness. As sissy babies, it is not uncommon to feel a sense of self-doubt and apprehension when it comes to embracing our sensual desires and fantasies. However, it is crucial to remember that these desires are a beautiful part of who we are, and it is essential to connect with them fully.

Self-consciousness often stems from societal expectations and judgments. We may fear being judged or misunderstood by others, leading us to suppress our deepest desires. The first step in overcoming self-consciousness is to recognize that our sensuality is valid and natural. It is a part of our authentic selves, and denying it only hinders our personal growth and fulfillment.

To begin this journey, let us focus on self-acceptance. Embracing our fantasies and desires starts with accepting ourselves unconditionally. Remember that there is no right or wrong when it comes to exploring sensuality, as long as it is consensual and brings joy to our lives. By accepting ourselves fully, we can start to shed the layers of self-consciousness that hold us back.

Another powerful tool in overcoming self-consciousness is meditation. Through guided meditations, we can connect with our inner desires and create a safe space for exploration. Meditation allows us to quiet the external noise and listen to our inner voices, enabling us to understand our fantasies on a deeper level. By regularly practicing meditation, we can cultivate a sense of peace, confidence, and self-assurance that helps us overcome self-consciousness.

Building a supportive community is equally important in our journey. Surrounding ourselves with like-minded individuals who understand and embrace their own sensuality can provide a safe and non-judgmental space for us to share our fantasies. This community can offer guidance, encouragement, and reassurance, reminding us that we are not alone in our desires.

Remember, dear sissy babies, the path to overcoming self-consciousness may not always be easy, but it is undoubtedly worth it. Embracing our fantasies and connecting with our sensual desires is a powerful act of self-love. As we navigate this journey, let us embrace our true selves, cultivate self-acceptance, practice meditation, and build a community that supports our growth. By doing so, we can break free from the shackles of self-consciousness and live a life of authentic sensuality and fulfillment.

Embracing Sensual Confidence

In the enchanting world of sensuality, where desires and fantasies come alive, lies a journey of self-discovery and empowerment for sissy babies. This subchapter, "Embracing Sensual Confidence," serves as a guiding light, illuminating the path towards embracing your deepest sensual desires and unlocking your true potential as a sissy baby.

Sensual confidence is not merely about physical appearance; it is a state of mind, an attitude that radiates from within. It is about embracing your unique sensuality and allowing yourself to revel in the intoxicating power of your fantasies. By connecting with your sensual desires, you can embark on a transformative journey that will enable you to fully embrace and celebrate your sissy identity.

Meditations for sissy babies to connect with their sensual desires and fantasies form the cornerstone of this chapter. Through these meditative practices, you will learn to quiet your mind, to go beyond societal expectations, and to delve deep into the recesses of your heart and soul. Allow yourself the freedom to explore your sensual desires without judgment or shame, for it is within this exploration that you will discover your true essence.

As a sissy baby, you are beautiful, unique, and deserving of love and acceptance. Embracing Sensual Confidence invites you to shed the chains of self-doubt and societal norms, and to embrace the sensuality that is inherent within you. By connecting with your sensual desires, you will tap into a wellspring of self-love and acceptance, allowing yourself to fully express your authentic self.

Throughout this subchapter, you will find a variety of exercises and practices designed to help you embrace your sensual confidence. From guided visualizations to affirmations and journaling prompts, each activity is carefully crafted to support your journey towards self-discovery and empowerment.

Remember, dear sissy baby, that your sensual desires and fantasies are a sacred part of who you are. Embrace them with open arms, for they hold the key to your true self. Through the meditations and practices outlined in this chapter, you will embark on a transformative journey towards self-acceptance, self-love, and sensual confidence. Embrace your fantasies, dear sissy baby, for they are the stepping stones to your ultimate liberation.

Finding Supportive Environments

In the journey of embracing your fantasies and connecting with your sensual desires as a sissy baby, it is crucial to seek out supportive environments. These spaces not only provide a safe haven for exploration but also offer the understanding and encouragement needed to fully embrace your authentic self. Finding such environments can be a transformative experience, propelling you towards self-acceptance and personal growth.

One of the first steps in finding supportive environments is to seek out like-minded individuals who share similar experiences and desires. Online communities and forums dedicated to sissy babies provide a virtual space where you can connect with others who understand and celebrate your fantasies. Here, you can share your thoughts, seek advice, and find the support you need to navigate your journey. These communities serve as a reminder that you are not alone in your desires and that there are others who share your journey.

Aside from online spaces, physical communities and support groups can also provide a nurturing environment for sissy babies. These groups often conduct regular meetups, workshops, and events where you can interact with others who are on a similar path. Engaging in face-to-face conversations and activities with individuals who understand and accept you can foster a sense of belonging and empowerment. Through these connections, you can find guidance and inspiration to further explore your sensual desires.

It is important to mention that finding supportive environments is a deeply personal process, and what works for one individual may not work for another. It may take time and effort to find the right community or group that aligns with your desires and values. Be patient and persistent in your search, and remember that the journey towards self-acceptance is a continuous one.

When you find a supportive environment, it is essential to nurture and maintain those connections. Engage actively in discussions, participate in events, and contribute to the community. By doing so, you not only help yourself but also contribute to the growth and support of others on similar journeys.

Remember, embracing your fantasies and connecting with your sensual desires as a sissy baby is a beautiful and valid part of your identity. Finding supportive environments will enable you to flourish and fully embrace your authentic self, surrounded by understanding, acceptance, and love.

www.ingramcontent.com/pod-product-compliance
Lightning Source LLC
Chambersburg PA
CBHW061007260726
48661CB00005B/2089